ROBERT CREELEY'S POETRY

Robert Creeley talking to his son Tom.   Dorfman

Cynthia Dubin Edelberg

ROBERT CREELEY'S POETRY

A Critical Introduction

UNIVERSITY OF NEW MEXICO PRESS

Albuquerque

© 1978 by the University of New Mexico Press. All rights reserved.
Library of Congress Catalog Card Number 78-55700.
International Standard Book Number 0-8263-0479-6.
Manufactured in the United States of America.
First edition

Excerpts from the works of Robert Creeley are reprinted with the permission of Charles Scribner's Sons and are fully protected by copyright.

"Helas," from *The Charm,* copyright © 1969 by Robert Creeley, reprinted by permission of Four Seasons Foundation.

Lines from "Often I Am Permitted To Return to A Meadow," from *The Opening of the Field,* copyright © 1960 by Robert Duncan, reprinted by permission of New Directions Publishing Corporation.

Library of Congress Cataloging in Publication Data

Edelberg, Cynthia Dubin, 1940–
  Robert Creeley's poetry.

  Bibliography: p. 181
  Includes index.
    1. Creeley, Robert, 1926–   —Criticism and interpretation.
I. Title.
PS3505.R43Z65   811'.5'4   78-55700
ISBN 0-8263-0479-6

For Stu

ACKNOWLEDGMENTS

In loving memory of my father, Jacob Dubin.

I would like to thank my family and friends for their enthusiasm during the good times and their patient love during the uncertain, especially my children, Jay, Jacqueline, and Wendy; my mother, Bertha Dubin Chaiten; and Stu Edelberg, David Dubin, Joan and Allan Beigel, Myra and Leonard Dinnerstein, and Myra and Alan Levenson. I am grateful indeed to Sidonie Smith, for her editorial advice, and to James Tuttleton and John Kuehl, for their confidence in my work.

CONTENTS

FOREWORD

Robert Creeley first became known as an influential and versatile writer associated with the legendary Black Mountain group. Now he is recognized as a central figure in contemporary American literature. Despite the fact that his poetic achievement is often the subject of critical attention, there has been no attempt to trace the development of his recurrent themes, or the modifications in his poetic posture, patterns of organization, and stylistic techniques. This study, the first full-length consideration of Creeley's poetry, explores the design of the whole by focusing on the most important poems in each of his major volumes to date (all of which have been published by Charles Scribner's Sons): *For Love: Poems 1950–1960* (1962), *Words* (1967), *Pieces* (1969), and *A Day Book* (1972). Any such interpretation of a work of art is personal and partial, necessarily. This analysis does not claim to be definitive; rather, the hope here is simply to contribute to a fuller understanding of a highly significant body of poetry.

Creeley's insights into the difficulties of Louis Zukofsky's work define the problem his own high-strung version of meditative poetry poses for the reader:

> In short, what Zukofsky has done is to take distinctions of both ear and intelligence to a fineness that is difficult. It is difficult to follow a man when he's thinking very closely. And it's extremely difficult to follow him when he's using all the resources that he has developed or inherited regarding the particular nature of words as sound.[1]

Creeley typically uses broken nervous lines to convey the sound of anxiety. This frantic sound serves to comment poignantly on the thematic emphasis in his earliest poems: the drama of the longed for dispassionate intelligence privately brooding on the intricacies of depressing thoughts. Disappointed in love and frustrated by words, he subordinates the emotional conflicts involved to his thoughts about his problems in cryptic poems the reader is permitted to overhear but apparently not always expected to understand. Taking his cue from the humanist viewpoint represented by Valéry's portrait of Monsieur Teste, Creeley based his rationale on the assumption that a preoccupation with the workings of the mind is the noblest activity, such acts of intellectual scrutiny being far removed from the insulting necessity of explanation. His detached posture is also a pose, however. It barely masks his altogether human need for a loving relationship with his wife and for satisfaction from his commitment to poetry. When his marriage ends, his calculatedly isolated stance is no match for the sadness and bitterness he feels. As the poems in *For Love*, Part II, attest, Creeley's compelling need to sort out the confusions of his life takes precedence over his compelling need to present a restrained, contemplative demeanor to the world. We get tension-filled poems in which he first confronts his feelings directly and then castigates himself for having betrayed his vulnerability in public. In general, the latest poems in *For Love* show Creeley expressing his feelings about love, thinking, and poetry in more straightforward fashion. In painfully brittle, nervous lines, which have become his trademark, he tells us about his awkward sense of love, his frustrations with the act of thinking, and about his tenuous faith in his poetic ability.

In *For Love*, which records a change of sensibility, Creeley begins by defining himself as an indifferent spectator of his own life and ends by acknowledging his passionate involvement with it. The poems in *Words* deal with this same process of transition. But in this volume, Creeley takes up these issues in comparatively explicit terms. He questions his basic assumption that the ideal exercise of the ideal mind could wring from ordinary experience its secret values. He concludes that analytical thinking, despite its inherent fascination, is of limited worth. He finds that his intuition is as reliable a guide in the world, that his spontaneous participation in the present moment is more worthwhile still. The poet wonders if even an ideal love relationship is enough to infuse his life with meaning and purpose. He decides that love is not the mystical panacea he once thought it to be but that love can be defined as a series of gratifications and disappointments. And, finally, he wonders if he will ever be able to control words in the precise way in which he would like to. His exploration of various aspects of this problem leads him to conclude that his failure or success as a poet in this sense is not the central issue. From the perspective of his own experience, making poems is simply a necessity.

Many of the poems in *Words* are organized around a thesis-antithesis-resolution structure, the same organizing principle that dominated *For Love*. However, in *Words*, especially in the later poems in the volume, Creeley experiments with other patterns. He offers us brief, impulsive poems, long, loosely associational poems, and "braided" poems in which he develops his three major themes simultaneously. By the time Creeley wrote *Pieces* he had attained facility with a diversity of poetic forms. In his first sequence, he binds different kinds of poetic statements together by using devices associated with the romance convention: a recognizable hero ponders his predicament and by implication our own by "descending" into three "areas" of his experience, taking counsel from wise, older poets who oversee the action, fighting a three-day mental battle with a sea monster, and enduring a nerve-wracking relationship with an "opaque" lady who, at the close of the sequence, rewards him for all that he has suffered and learned.

Although the deliberately contrived framework that shapes *Pieces* overall signals a departure from *For Love* and *Words*, which conveyed merely a sense of sequence, Creeley is concerned in *Pieces* with the same themes that engaged his attention in the previous volumes. Earlier, he debated and ultimately qualified the promise of the intellect, the power of love, and the purpose of poetry. Now, he is less innocent about his motivations and expectations. His sophisticated mode of perception, more accurately *apperception*, is based on a fusion of the analytical and the intuitive assessment, and on a realization, reluctantly grasped, that love is not a beatific force but a complex, working bond between people. His seasoned way of perceiving experience is also based on an awareness that the poet does not have a special gift which assures him insight into the truth of the ordinary but rather that the poet is destined to tell "the story I/ myself knew only the way of" as best he can. Creeley brings his more realistic attitudes to bear on the "small facts," the "breathtaking banalities" of his life in an attempt to understand their significance. He discovers that his new mode of apperception is unequal to the task of unraveling life's mysteries.

"In London," a travel sequence made up of loosely connected observations welded together by the rhythm of life as Creeley actually lived it from November 1968, to June 1971, takes up the same issues explored in *Pieces*. By the close of *Pieces*, Creeley seemed content with the existentialist viewpoint, which offered no escape from the unexplainable contradictions of life. But in "In London," his need to feel at home with himself and at home in the world is sharpened and intensified by his fear of death. He continues to probe the question that nags at him persistently: *"What law/ or/ mystery// is involved?"* He wants "to find something/ worthy of respect" which in turn will help "to/ get all the confusions at last/ resolved." The poems in this sequence follow the traveler on his way home to Bolinas, California, at the same time that they follow him on his way "home" to death. He finds that he is unable to settle on a believable "something" that will both mitigate his fear of dying and lend unshakable purpose to his life. Instead, he takes comfort from fleeting moments of serenity—time spent with loved friends usually in a natural setting—as a substitute for the meta-physical reassurance that he has a "place" in what he would like to be convinced is an eternally alive "All." Creeley neither proposes a method for achieving serenity nor discusses this treasured, elusive moment in technical, religious terms, as many writers who have recently come under the Buddhist influence have done. Neither a theologian nor a philosopher, he presents the peaceful scene without comment, depending on its unique character in the company of poems about restlessness, fear, and despair to bespeak his conclusion to date: on the rare occasion when he can abandon himself to the pleasures of fellowship and to the beauty of the physical world, life, despite its tragic nature, makes sense to him.

INTRODUCTION

In an unpublished autobiographical note written in 1966, Robert Creeley talks about the tragedies that shaped his childhood:

> I was raised in Massachusetts for the most part, having been born in Arlington, May 21, 1926, son of a physician who died when I was four. That and the loss of my left eye when I was a little younger mark for me two conditions I have unequivocally as content, but which I have neither much bitterness about nor other specific feeling. I did miss my father certainly. With him went not only the particular warmth he might have felt for me, but also the whole situation of our life as we had apparently known it.[1]

Dr. Oscar Creeley had been a prominent physician, and his death altered his son's "situation" considerably. Creeley grew up on a small farm in West Acton that his father had bought to serve as a quiet country home.[2] His mother, a reserved woman who was Dr. Creeley's third wife, worked as a public health nurse to support Robert and his older sister, Helen.[3] Because his mother was "distracted" by her commitment to earn a living, Creeley turned to their housekeeper, an impoverished, inarticulate immigrant his father had rescued from a state home for the mentally retarded. He describes her as the "emotional center" of his early life.[4] Although in retrospect he feels that it took him "a curiously long time to come into a man's estate"[5] because he was raised in a fatherless household, that he "always came on too strong to people casually met"[6] because he grew up in relative isolation, and that he was particularly vulnerable because he had a glass eye,[7] Creeley looks back to his childhood as a generally happy period in his life.[8] One of his fondest memories is of the woods in West Acton: "I could go out into those woods and feel completely open. I mean, all the kinds of dilemmas that I would feel sometimes would be resolved by going out into the woods. . . ."[9]

Creeley was awarded a scholarship to Holderness School in

Plymouth, New Hampshire. This school, he recalls, "was so generous in its understanding" that he feels the "most relevant" part of his education was the time he spent there.[10] His experience at Harvard was less satisfactory: "I found little place despite the various friendships I made [with John Hawkes, Mitchell Goodman, Seymour Lawrence and Jacob Leed, among others]. Only one teacher, Fred McCreary, gave me any sense that I might have possibility as a writer."[11] By late 1944 his life, as he phrases it now, was "rapidly deteriorating." He had been suspended from Harvard for stealing a door from Lowell House, his relationship with Ann MacKinnon, who would become his first wife, was chaotic, and his job as a copy boy in Boston was intolerably tedious. He welcomed an American Field Service assignment as an ambulance driver in India as a "great adventure," a liberation from Cambridge, Massachusetts.[12]

When the war was over, Creeley returned to Cambridge, where his family was then living. His feelings about his family and his education had been ambivalent before he went to India; by the time he returned his sense of alienation was intensified by what he characterizes as a pervasive restlessness: "Everyone was looking for where it was happening and desperately wanted to be accepted by it, because frankly the society as it then was, coming back from the war and realizing home and mother just wasn't no matter how lovely, any great possibility."[13]

Creeley felt cut off from "the society as it then was." "Return," written during the winter of 1945, was the first of his poems to be published. In it, he expresses his relief at finding his "door" on an otherwise "endless" street and, simultaneously, his sense of feeling apart.

Return

Quiet as is proper for such places;
The street, subdued, half-snow, half-rain,
Endless, but ending in the darkened doors.
Inside, they who will be there always,
Quiet as is proper for such people—
Enough for now to be here, and
To know my door is one of these.[14]

The first five lines of the poem sketch a cold, dark insular society of "quiet" places and people "who will be there always." Repetition and alliteration suggest a rigidly patterned, predictable circumstance to which the poet almost, but not quite, belongs. The dash ending line 5 separates the speaker from "such places" and "such people." Furthermore, his "door" should be "one of those" to satisfy the expectation set up by the sound of "know," but, it turns out, his "door" is "one of these." Formally, there is at least one word in each line of "Return" which anticipates the sound of the final word in the line—"as is" : "Places"; "half-snow" : "half-rain"; "darkened" : "doors"; "They" : "always"; "proper" : "people"; "Enough for now" : "and." "These," the last word of "Return," designates the poet's "place," which is conspicuously alone.

When Creeley returned from the American Field Service, he was reinstated at Harvard. Looking for "where it was happening," he became involved in the activities surrounding the publication of *Wake*, a magazine started by Harvard undergraduates the year before as an alternative to the Harvard *Advocate*, a publication Creeley and his friends felt was misguidedly sympathetic to the New Criticism. He was the associate editor for the Cummings issue (Spring 1946), which published "Return." His friendship with the editors of *Wake* led to the publication of several other of his early poems as well. But more important, according to Mary Novik, whose biographical sketch is the most complete account to date of Creeley's life, "*Wake* was for Creeley virtually the only example of an alternative little magazine dedicated to the publication of new writing, however ephemeral. It was with this audience in mind that he first began seriously to write and to identify himself as a writer."[15]

For Creeley, the jazz clubs around Boston provided another alternative to "society as it then was": "This was the time of the whole cult of the hipster" and Charlie Parker was "the hero of that possibility."[16] The form of Parker's improvisational compositions derived from the unique flux of the immediately felt experience which prompted the music. Although it would be years before Creeley could do so himself, he learned from the jazz cult that "you can write directly from that which you feel." These musicians, who experimented with rhythm and silence, showed him "how *subtle*" and "how *refined* that expression might be."[17] In his preface to *All That Is Lovely in Men* (a slim volume published in 1955 and later incorporated, in part, into *For Love*) Creeley acknowledges his debt:

line-wise, the most complementary sense I have found is that of musicians like Charlie Parker, and Miles Davis. I am interested in how that is done, how "time" there is held to a measure peculiarly an evidence (a hand) of the emotion which prompts (drives) the poem in the first place.[18]

Against the background of these restless times, Creeley married Ann in the spring of 1946. It was a tense relationship from the start. Ten years later it ended in a bitter divorce. Thinking back to the spring of 1946 from the vantage point of the present, Creeley tries to understand his decision to marry:

> One of the sad dilemmas of that time was that the content of that war experience was in no way locatable among the people of my life. I remember not long after going over to see if I could relocate an old girlfriend at Radcliffe. I came in this battle dress and I'm sort of given a charming flash response from these young ladies. I'm wearing a black patch at that time and I looked kind of dramatic. Well, again, it was useless to me. I really wanted something to locate me. I've been through this extraordinary chaotic time. It isn't that I felt I was owed anything but my college background up to that point had already been dislocating. My relation with my family was warm and emotionally good but it was that characteristic dilemma of inability not because they didn't want to understand what it was that I wanted to do or what I thought I had as a possibility or what I really had in mind to accomplish. To add to the chaos of being a college student at that time was now this whole war scene which you couldn't report to people. I didn't feel smug—like, you people don't know what I went through. I didn't feel any drama or heroism but I felt I can't get these two realities to be in the same world and, even more to the point, I can't find my own situation as relates to either one.
>
> I did literally locate this girl who was as dislocated as I was. Really I all but—no, I don't think I forced her to marry me. I think we had the mutual need for somebody to locate so we grabbed on to each other. I think I really did insist upon marriage just to be real, to take up a real role as I assumed it to be.[19]

The Creeleys moved to Provincetown, Massachusetts, shortly

after their marriage. They came to the bohemian community on the strength of Creeley's friendship with Slater Brown, a writer and one-time friend of E. E. Cummings, Allen Tate, Malcolm Cowley, and Hart Crane. Brown had fascinating stories to tell, and he encouraged Creeley's decision to become a writer.[20] But living in Provincetown had its drawbacks. Creeley left Harvard shortly before graduation because the open-bar commute on the ferry to and from Cambridge proved a distraction. And, too, he began to feel that the course work was useless to him. After a year in Provincetown, the Creeleys moved to a farm near Littleton, New Hampshire, where he spent his time reading, writing, and breeding pigeons for exhibition (an interest of his since childhood). It was at this point that Creeley initiated his lengthy correspondence with Charles Olson.

The Creeley-Olson letters were especially important in strengthening Creeley's resolve to pursue a literary career. They began shortly after Creeley heard Richard Wilbur read his own poems on Cid Corman's radio program, "This Is Poetry." He wrote to Corman (and to Ezra Pound and William Carlos Williams, who also responded) asking about potential contributors for a planned literary magazine. The magazine was to be a sympathetic outlet for new writing "free of the current imposition of the literary hierarchy,"[21] an alternative to the *Hudson Review* and *Kenyon Review*. Corman put Creeley in touch with Vincent Ferrini, who had gathered several of Olson's poems for his own periodical and sent them on. Creeley replied to Ferrini: "To tell the truth, I'm rather put off by Mr. Olson's language which doesn't seem to come to any kind of positive diction. . . . there's the looking around for a language, and the result is a loss of force."[22] Then Olson to Creeley—to whom he would dedicate *The Maximus Poems:*

> my dear robert creeley;
>   so Bill W. too says, write creeley, he
> has ideas and wants to USE 'em
>   so what do i do? so i write so ferrini
> sends creeley a lovely liquid thing and creeley
> says, he's a boll weevil, olson, just a lookin'
> for a lang, just a lookin' nuts, and i says,
> creeley, you're off yer trolley; a man
> god damn well has to come up with his own lang.,

syntax and song both, but also each poem under
hand has its own language, which is variant of
same. (THIS IS THE BATTLE: i wish
    very much, creeley, i had now to send
    you what PNY publishes summer issue
    PROjective Verse vs the Non-projective:
    the argument pitches here
                  (I've dubbed
    the alternative to composing by inherited
    forms "composition by field"—it needs
    more examination than I give it in
    that kickoff piece))[23]

When the Creeley-Olson exchange of letters began during the
spring of 1950, Olson had not yet completed "Projective Verse" or
written "Human Universe," his seminal essays, or *The Maximus
Poems,* his three-volume sequence; he had, however, been thinking
seriously about poetic composition for a long time. When Olson
was Director of Foreign Nationalities Division of the Democratic
National Committee in Washington, D.C., he often visited Pound
in St. Elizabeth's Hospital ("Olson saved my life")[24] and talked
with him about "projective" poetry, which many observers of contemporary perspectives in literature, like Michael Reck, Pound's
biographer, feel "derived from Pound anyhow."[25] Olson passed
along to Creeley in a barrage of letters the substance of his much
discussed ideas about making the line a true register of a poet's
individual speech pattern and thought process. This process of
clarification was mutually profitable. Creeley recalls:

> And then those letters actually became incorporated finally in
> that essay on projective verse—in the first section, where he is
> talking about the significance of the syllable, the sense of
> breathing, the sense of where the intelligence is operating and
> the choice of the language where the whole physiology of man
> is at work in the poem.[28]

Creeley says he learned from those letters to make the length of the
line reflect the stress complex that compelled it because, as he says,
Olson "started to show me where habits and attitudes toward the
line were really not only blocking the particular emotional
intensity that I was working for, but he showed me how the whole

way of speech was not true to the way I was thinking."[27] In other words, Olson helped Creeley to find his own voice: "Olson, I believe, was a decisive influence upon me as a writer, because he taught me how to write. Not how to write poems that he wrote, but how to write poems that I write. This is a very curious and specific difference."[28]

Olson insisted that the line of the poem truly record the poet's actual speech pattern. He convinced Creeley that the end-stopped line he had used in "Return" was artificial because no one speaks consistently in complete sentences. Olson went further than proposing a theory of composition. When Creeley sent him poems in manuscript form, Olson either suggested ways in which the line might be changed or he changed the line himself. Therefore, it is not altogether possible to know which poet's voice we hear in Creeley's earlier poems. The poem "Helas" is a case in point.

Creeley wrote "Helas" in February 1951, and sent it to Olson for comment. "Helas" shows Creeley entering the world of letters as an *eiron*, the stock character of Greek comedy. This pose enables him to make outrageous use of techniques, words, and interests associated with Olson, Pound, and Williams. But "Helas" ends unconventionally with a final irony; having exposed and exploited the flaws of his mentors, Creeley finds himself defeated at the end of the poem by essentially the same problem he had at the start: "The shapes of light [sacred words]/ have surrounded the senses,/ but will not take them to hand."

helas

Helas! Or Christus fails.
The day is indefinite. The shapes of light
have surrounded the senses,
but will not take them to hand (as would an axe-edge
take to its stone . . .)

It is not a simple bitterness that comes between.
Worn by these simplicities, the head
revolves, turns in the wind but lacks
its delight.

What, now, more than sight
or sound could compel it, drive, new,
these mechanics for compulsion

                                        (nothing else but
          to bite home! there, where
          the head could take hold . . .)

                                        which are vague,
              in the wind,
          take no edge from the wind, no edge
          or delight?

                                                              (p. 20)

   "Helas" is based on Williams's "The Wind Increases," which
Creeley quotes directly in the second parenthetical passage:
"(nothing else but/ to bite home! there where/ the head could take
hold . . .)." When the letters between Creeley and Olson are
published they will show that Olson put in the parentheses around
"as would an axe-edge/ take to its stone . . ." but did not explain
his motive. Without the parentheses, the phrase suggests a comfortable and purposeful action connected with farming. With the
parenthesis, the phrase is by association, a literary allusion. It is, in
fact, a quotation from Olson's poem "La Torre," also written in
1951. Thus "Helas" implies that Olson's voice is as important as
Williams's. In effect, Olson changed the meaning of Creeley's
poem. Perhaps "Helas" is an extreme instance. Yet it raises
questions that might be answered when the Creeley-Olson correspondence is published. To what extent did Olson suggest alternative patterns of lining? To what extent did he actually put into
Creeley's poems Cummings-inspired devices of presentation that
were also identified with his own technique, such as open
parentheses, variant spellings like *thot, wd, cd,* broken sentences,
and unconventional spacing? To what extent did he alter Creeley's
meaning? And, finally, to what extent was Creeley aware of this ?
   The voluminous Creeley-Olson correspondence during the early
fifties—at one point Creeley calculated he "was spending a full
eight hours a day writing them"[29]—was typical of the way in which
most of the poets first associated with Corman's *Origin* and later
with Creeley's *Black Mountain Review* managed their relationships
through the mails. For instance, the published portion of Olson's
letters to Corman, which have chiefly to do with the events leading
up to Corman's final editing and publication of *Origin* I, devoted to
Olson's work, and *Origin* II (July 1951), "featuring Robert
Creeley," give us insight into the working of this vast network of

communication through which, Creeley says, the poets began "to realize" themselves, "to get location, to realize what other writers were particular to our own discriminations."[30] These friends wrote about aesthetic theory. They reviewed each other's work. They exchanged comments about editorial policy and the logistics of publication.

The letters about the difficulties involved in finding sympathetic publishers led Creeley to establish the Divers Press in Mallorca which began by issuing *Origin* III in the spring of 1953:

> I wanted a press that would be of use to specific people, *including* myself. I printed two of my own books [*A Snarling Garland of Xmas Verses* and *The Kind of Act of*], two of Blackburn's and I printed Olson [*Mayan Letters*], Irving Layton [*In the Midst of My Fever* and *The Blue Propeller*] and so on. We had to. We had to have the dignity of our own statement. We had to have it in a form that could be available to other people.[31]

Perhaps the most life-ordering significance these thousands of letters held for Creeley was of a personal nature. Olson invited him to teach at Black Mountain College and to edit *Black Mountain Review* as a result of the relationship they initiated and sustained solely through their correspondence.

By 1954 Olson was an established figure at Black Mountain College. This experimental college in North Carolina, founded by John Andrew Rice in 1933, began under the influence of John Dewey: the faculty worked "to understand the community" with "everybody participating" in the application of Dewey's social ethic.[32] The school also survived the next influx of teachers who came during the late thirties and were more concerned with the "functional concept of the arts and of the organization of the intelligence generally." This spirit continued to dominate the college after Josef Albers, the director, left Black Mountain in the late forties to become the head of the Yale School of Design. Olson's association with the school began in 1945 when he commuted back and forth from his government job in Washington, D.C., to Black Mountain College to take over his friend Edward Dahlberg's teaching position. He became rector in 1951 and in that capacity saw the college through its final days in 1957. Under his direction the school was owned and operated by the teaching body, a group made up of people intimately associated with some creative activity (Franz Kline, John Cage, Merce Cunningham, Willem de Kooning, Paul Goodman, among others) who were expected to share their experience with students who were similarly involved. The promise was compromised by the reality; Black Mountain College was unaccredited and, more important, it was on the verge of bankruptcy.

By 1954 Olson was struggling to keep the college alive. He decided that if Black Mountain had thirty-five students, fifteen more than actually enrolled, it could be self-supporting. He hit on the idea of *Black Mountain Review.* Olson hoped this promotional publication would be the most effective yet least expensive way of reaching people who might be interested in a Black Mountain education. Cid Corman wanted to be its editor. Because he and Olson were close friends, Corman had reason to expect the job. More to the point, he had devoted *Origin* I entirely to Olson's work and he made virtually every subsequent issue available to Olson as well. Nonetheless, Olson chose Creeley, the poet he said was "worth more than all the rest of us," the writer he said he "learned more from . . . than from any living man."[33] In a letter to Corman (December 14, 1954) Olson speaks about his decision and about the projected format of *Black Mountain Review:*

> The point is,
> i hope i am the first to tell you that Robt is coming here as of March 29th, not only as an addition to the faculty in writing, but as editor of a new quarterly, to be called "The Black Mt. Quarterly, 100 pages, big review section, and planned to compete with Kenyon, Partisan, NMQ (what else is there, are Hudson & Sewanee, still in existence?) Anyway, that sort of thing. And with a circulation of 2500 to be shot at. Also, To carry ads.[34]

While Olson was wrestling with the problems facing Black Mountain, the Creeleys were living on the Spanish island of Mallorca with their three young children. From the start of their marriage they lived on a small income Ann received from a trust fund. This financial imbalance generated a particular kind of tension Creeley often refers to in his writing. As he put it in a letter to Williams: "I was going to be a writer, and we lived on 215 a month she got from a trust fund. . . . Embarrassed continually, that I did not 'support' her and the children— but equally endlessly covetous and anxious of the time it gave me."[35]

"Embarrassed continually" yet "endlessly covetous," Creeley defended his usefulness by admitting inadequacy and then capitalizing on the confession. Although it seems contradictory, self-effacement is an effective weapon in the hands of a skilled practitioner of negative power, as Creeley's first published story, "The Unsuccessful Husband," demonstrates. The "businesses" the husband "so carefully guided into failure" are presented as evidence of his well-meaning determination to satisfy his cruelly insensitive wife. The Creeleys' life in Mallorca (November 1952 to March 1954) is the subject of *The Island*, his only novel. Again, the husband is unsuccessful, financially dependent on his wife, and quick to say *mea culpa*. As Creeley's poetry and prose of the early fifties make plain, his marriage was on the verge of collapse. He was looking for a viable alternative; the idea of a job at Black Mountain was an attractive possibility. He quickly accepted Olson's offer to join the writing faculty and to edit the magazine.

The first issue of *Black Mountain Review* (Spring 1954) was printed on Mallorca by the Divers Press just before Creeley left his home there to teach at the College from March to July 1954. Although Creeley had twice before planned to edit a magazine, he never actually did and he knew practically nothing about teaching. Olson had, quite simply, rescued his intellectually stimulating friend from a difficult time in his marriage. Creeley recalls:

> I didn't meet Olson, until I went to teach at Black Mountain in 1954—which job saved my life in many ways, and certainly changed it altogether. Living in Mallorca, despite the ease and beauty of the place, I'd begun to feel I was literally good for nothing—and Olson's offer of a job, and equally his giving me the magazine to edit, changed that subject completely.[36]

In July 1955, Creeley returned to Mallorca to find, sadly, that his relationship with Ann could not be reconciled. Olson rescued him a second time by asking him to teach at Black Mountain for the fall term. Again, Black Mountain was "a place to *go*."[37] Ann left Mallorca shortly after she supervised the printing of Duncan's *Caesar's Gate*, the last publication by the Divers Press. Creeley taught at Black Mountain until January 1956, when Robert Duncan came and took over his responsibilities. The Creeleys were

divorced in New York during the winter of 1956. In a letter to
William Carlos Williams dated August 8, 1956, Creeley says that
shortly after this painful and bitter divorce he went west on a "poor
man's odyssey" to search for the "means to my supposed
redemption."[38]

Creeley went west, stopping first in Albuquerque, New Mexico,
and finally on to San Francisco, where he met Allen Ginsberg, Gary
Snyder, Philip Whalen, Kenneth Rexroth, and Philip Lamatia,
among others. He put together samplings of their work for *Black
Mountain Review*, No. 7, the final issue of the magazine. In this
way Creeley became part of the San Francisco "renaissance." His
"poor man's odyssey" was worthwhile for still another reason. He
returned to Albuquerque, where, in January 1957, he met and
within two weeks married Bobbie Louise Hall.

At the time Bobbie Hall had two daughters, Kirsten and Leslie.
In the two years that followed, the Creeleys had two more
daughters, Sarah and Katherine. A sense of family, a teaching job at
a small day-school for boys in Albuquerque, and graduate work at
the University of New Mexico, taken together, gave Creeley a
measure of stability in his life that he had lacked for some time.
The tone of the poetry he wrote during the late fifties reflects that
change accordingly. By the sixties, the urgency and despair that
had, either explicitly or by implication, marked his earliest work
yielded to a more composed mood and a more philosophical
purview.

At the same time that Creeley's personal life was settling into a
more manageable style, his professional life was becoming more
secure. Although his work had been admired by the poets
associated with *Origin* and *Black Mountain Review*, the appearance of his poems in *Poetry* made his work available to a wider
reading public and opened the way for academic acceptance. In
fact, an account of Creeley's recognition by *Poetry* magazine
during these years provides a convenient index by which his
increasing stature as a poet can be measured. In August 1957, his
first poem appeared in *Poetry*. In the May 1958 edition of this journal, Louis Zukofsky reviewed Creeley's *The Whip*, a collection of
thirty-eight poems culled from the earlier slim volumes. In April of
1959, eight poems appeared in *Poetry*, and in May 1960, ten new
poems were published for which Creeley received the Levinson
Prize. The June 1964 issue of *Poetry* brought out thirteen new
poems, which won him the Levinson-Blumenthal Prize.

Aside from being a prolific writer during the last twenty years, Creeley has been an active member of the literary community. He has participated in many writers' workshops and poetry conferences; the Vancouver Poetry Festival (Summer 1963) and the Berkeley Poetry Conference (Summer 1965) were perhaps the most significant. Creeley has taught in a variety of places including a finca in Guatemala, the University of New Mexico, the University of British Columbia, and the State University of New York at Buffalo. In April 1964, he read with Robert Duncan and Denise Levertov at the Guggenheim Museum in New York, and since that time he has read at virtually every major university in the United States and Britain. He often joined other writers in their protest against the Vietnam war though he did not take up this issue in his poetry.

In 1970, the Creeleys moved to Bolinas, California, a community of artists and writers. A sampling of work by poets who identify themselves with Bolinas can be found in *On the Mesa: An Anthology of Bolinas Writing* (San Francisco: City Lights, 1971). On the back cover of this volume, the editors explain: "Several divergent movements in American poetry of the past 20 years (Black Mountain, San Francisco Beat, 'New York School' of poets) have come together with new Western and mystic elements at the unpaved crossroads of Bolinas." In poems written during his years in Bolinas, Creeley refers to it as a literal place in which he and his family live and as a mystical place in which he finds a profound sense of peace and wonder.

Creeley's poetry deserves careful and serious attention, as many critics have testified. Hugh Kenner judges Creeley to be "one of the very few contemporaries with whom it is essential to keep one's acquaintance current."[39] Kenneth Rexroth, ranking the poets who have come into prominence since World War II, places him "second only to Denise Levertov."[40] Richard Howard refers to his "status of a *chef d'école*";[41] and Robert Duncan mentions "the excellence of Creeley's art in poetry" as a foregone conclusion.[42] There are critics, however, who are unable to find a single redeeming feature in his poetry. For John Corrington, *"For Love* is clear and present evidence that Robert Creeley is one of the most exorbitantly overrated poets practicing today." He is amazed that Creeley's "admirers—and they seem to be legion—will not have it so."[43] John Simon concurs with Corrington: "There are two things to be said about Creeley's poems: they are short; they are not short enough."[44]

Most of the critics who have tried to ascertain Creeley's position in contemporary American literature have addressed themselves to specific issues apropos of his poetry as well. Two major points of controversy concern Creeley's use of the common speech idiom and his poetic posture. Kenner praises his "often miraculous control of spoken American."[45] Rexroth notes that "his poetry is distinguished by a remarkable sensitivity to the inflections of speech."[46] According to Donald Hall, Creeley renders "colloquial speech with accuracy and a fine sense of proportion";[47] and William Carlos Williams describes his phrasing as "the subtlest feeling for measure that I encounter anywhere except in the verses of Ezra Pound."[48] Ian Hamilton and M. L. Rosenthal disagree. Hamilton explains that it is Creeley's intention "to write a poetic language that is distinctively American." But, he goes on, "if we are not tuned in, too bad—we will be left with something, stuttering, short-winded, flat and, if he says so, thoroughly American."[49] Rosenthal complains that Creeley often "exploits our modern openness to the colloquial tone in poetry." He faults him for offering us "loose and stumbling casualness" as a substitute for the effective and satisfying "assimilation of natural speech."[50] Kenneth Cox does not object to Creeley's handling of colloquial speech, but he does suggest that "it is intended to camouflage a posture which should be studied in terms of its relation to late medieval love poetry."[51]

Cox raises a question about Creeley's poetic "posture," an issue which has also become a subject of critical controversy. Louis Zukofsky speaks about Creeley's poetry in terms of sincerity, a key word for Zukofsky. He discerns an "honest metaphysical intention" at its core; this "one fact moves all of his poems."[52] Gilbert Sorrentino says flatly: "I love the man's work because of the honesty of its own darkness, my failing perhaps."[53] And Jerome Mazzaro finds that Creeley's poetry approaches the accuracy demanded by John Ruskin of the ideal poet in *Modern Painters* because his poetry reveals "an honesty that is not easily gained."[54] Other critics challenge this sincerity. Hamilton thinks Creeley an "unremittingly self-conscious writer" who has "one eye on the audience."[55] William Dickey interprets Creeley's poetic posture as one of calculated reticence although he is at a loss to interpret its purpose: "If this reluctance of Creeley's to let things emerge from hiding is a poetic principle, I do not understand its value for the poems that are successful here [*For Love*] are the ones that contradict it."[56]

Both Creeley's poetic "posture" and his pacing of the line are more complex aspects of his work than critics have so far indicated in their brief studies. Indeed, it is difficult to make general statements about Creeley's poetry that are both useful and valid. A close examination of any one of his volumes reveals a wide range of personal attitudes and methods of expression. In *For Love,* for instance, Creeley uses an impressive variety of poetic voices, only one of which strikes the note of colloquial ease. In other poems he sounds nervous or hesitant—conspicuously antiidiomatic—and in still other poems he uses "Elizabethanisms," and in still others, childish pratter. Similarly, Creeley's poetic stance changes often even in the course of a single volume. Now he is shy, now arrogant, now poignant, now contemptuous. Thus it is of limited value to speak of a typical Creeley poem. His leap from genre to genre in his other literary work may dramatize the fact that Creeley does not stay with one technique, voice, or viewpoint in his poetry in any systematic sense: one editorship, *Black Mountain Review;* one collection of short stories, *The Gold Diggers;* one novel, *The Island;* one collection of critical notes, *A Quick Graph;* one collection of interviews, *Contexts of Poetry;* one radio play, *Listen;* one long essay on "The Creative."

Yet a third problem arises in a study of Creeley's poetry. It is difficult to read his poems without preconceived expectations. Most critics refer to Creeley as a Black Mountain writer and mention his indebtedness to Olson and "Projective Verse." The commonly held assumption—Olson was the master and Creeley the disciple—often blocks an awareness of what Creeley was and was not trying to do in his poetry. The name Black Mountain has little significance as a definition of literary style: "none of the so-called Black Mountain writers wrote in a literally similar manner."[57] Creeley has complained that "Black Mountain" is used in too general a fashion:

"So I almost would like—not to bury Black Mountain, because it probably gave me more coherence than I otherwise would have had, certainly that, but I don't like to feel that it's any exclusion, or any ultimate purpose of form or via that's finally been settled upon once and for all."[58]

On the one hand it is clear from even a brief summary of Creeley's life that Olson was more instrumental than anyone else in helping him find a place in the literary world. His hundreds of letters to Creeley were filled with provocative comments about aesthetic theory and concrete suggestions for refining specific poems. These letters, Creeley has written, "were of such energy and calculation that they constituted a practical 'college' of stimulus and information."[59] Moreover, by appointing him to the faculty of Black Mountain College, Olson involved Creeley in a sympathetic community of productive writers and artists. By appointing him editor of *Black Mountain Review*, he gave him a responsibility which made him a central figure in that community and, at the same time, made it possible for him to establish relationships easily with writers elsewhere, most notably in the San Francisco area.

On the other hand, it has been a mistake to overestimate Olson's influence on Creeley's poetry itself. Olson described the poet's job in terms of spontaneity: "fronting the whole front of reality as it now presents itself"[60] and, simultaneously, articulating the "fronting" process: "(The distinction here is between language as the act of the instant and language as the act of thought about the instant.)"[61] Olson's method for conveying the feeling of immediacy, like Jack Kerouac's "spontaneous prose," André Breton's "automatic writing," and Jackson Pollock's "action painting," depends on the seasoned artist's ability to make split-second decisions about his medium in the first place and on his confident willingness to stand by his unrevised product in the last. By contrast, Creeley valued intelligent, deliberative self-scrutiny, both for the sake of its inherent fascination as well as for the promise of life-controlling wisdoms such thinking and rethinking implied. Although many of his early poems look like the work of a "projectivist" poet because they contain devices of presentation associated with Olson, they are essentially thesis-antithesis "idea" poems written by an unpracticed poet who admired Wallace Stevens and, more crucially, Paul Valéry.

In fact, *Monsieur Teste*, Valéry's manual of "conscious consciousness," to use Emily Dickinson's apt words, was Creeley's bible from the late forties until he rejected it in the mid sixties. Thus, a familiarity with Teste's "system of self-awareness" can help us understand Creeley's poetic posture, sequence of thought, and vocabulary in the most fascinating of his early poems collected in

For Love, many of which show that he identifies with Monsieur Teste. In his middle poems collected in *Words,* Creeley reconsiders the worth of Teste's "system"; and, finally, in his recent sequences, *Pieces* and "In London" (*A Day Book*), he refers to Teste's "system" (though he does not name it) as a contrived posture of self-sufficiency he once believed would protect him from the vicissitudes of life but one which he has come to realize thwarts his unanalyzable, overwhelming need to feel a sense of belonging in the world.

Monsieur Teste is the "completed mind" committed to studying its own structure and operation.[62] By virtue of "incomparable intellectual gymnastics," Teste attempts "the complete realization of Self with regard to the given" and thus, at every moment, can reflect on the fundamental question: "What is man's potential?" Specifically, Teste divides the world into what he knows and "all the rest." The challenge of the unknown, of what he "cannot manage to think," spurs his existence, is his existence. The "object-of-knowledge" under Teste's scrutiny is relevant only in that it stimulates him to think through to a definitive statement about it. Since "there is rarely a thought free of the sense that it is provisional," the possibility that he will catch the *"knowing-knowledge* moment" is indeed remote. If by chance he should, the "thing understood is finished"; Teste must then focus on another "indifferent fact" with his "strange power of thinking-sensibility," or he too will be finished. It is crucial that Teste bring to this "activity an extraordinary amount of energy, of willed profundity" so that "his whole being" is "concentrated in a certain *place* on the frontiers of consciousness." Completely absorbed and completely alone, Teste exists in a "privileged region" in space and time—"That point of *inner* civilization where consciousness . . . finds its repose (if this be repose) only in the sense of its own miracles, its own exercise, its own substitutes, and its innumerable distinctions." Encased "in the armor of his own image," Teste pursues "the knowing-knowledge moment" dispassionately: "This thing could count the buttons on a hangman's coat. . . ." Contemptuous of his feelings, "he stirred his passions when he willed" in order to "dominate" and "despise" them. Contemptuous of his thoughts, he surrounds them with a "retinue of qualifications" or creates *"another self"* to do the same. And so Teste, "a man *camped* in his life. . . . wholly given to his inner practices his profound prey," can go on forever.

Teste assumes that the mind, in conversation with itself,

constitutes the most special occasion. Although he is *"able* to produce, as well as anyone, in one genre or another," he feels no need to communicate: "I am at home in MYSELF, I speak my own language. . . ." Teste is so certain he will be judged unintelligible that he actually permits himself in a gleeful moment to issue a challenge to his readers:

> And I shall be the prize of this riddle. I shall make myself known to those who solve the puzzle of the universe and have sufficient contempt for the organs and other means I have invented to conclude against their evidence and against their own clear thought.[63]

Not every one of Creeley's poems need be considered in these terms, but many of his so-called obscure poems become clear when we recognize that they are patterned on Teste's "system of self-awareness." Nonetheless, poems based on unfamiliar assumptions are bound to be confusing. Creeley has recognized that some of his early work "has been felt to be so exclusively personal that people question its relevance to others"; he explains that in his later work he has tried "to strip away all that kind of qualification" so that the emphasis is on the common essence of the personally experienced occasion and not on the private situation itself.[64] To understand the general direction Creeley's poetry takes as well as the individual poems which are reference points along the way, this study must begin by asking why he felt drawn to the Monsieur Teste pose.

1

FOR LOVE:
POEMS 1950–1960

"What caused the fall of the angels
is the contrary of what caused and
still causes the fall of man.

They fell because they had no heart—
and man, for love."

—Paul Valéry

The fundamental assumption of Robert Creeley's finest early poetry is that the mind, in conversation with itself, constitutes an always necessary and sometimes special occasion. The central ordering events of his own childhood—the death of his father and the loss of his left eye—made him acutely aware that survival in the world depends on tracing clearly the nature of one's own experience. Determined to be self-reliant, he cultivated a habit of taking nothing for granted, of surrounding a possibility, any possibility, with a battery of qualifications. From the vantage point of middle age, Creeley reflected on the deliberately cautious way in which he protected his supposed vulnerability by assessing and reassessing the immediate significance and even unlikely implications of whatever he was "given":

> I knew that something whipped me constantly in my own experience of things. Something was really, you know, WHAM, WHAM, slashing and cutting me. And yet if I walked down the street I knew that nobody was coming at me in that fashion, so where in the name of heaven was all this taking place? Well, it was taking place in my thinking. Someone would hand me something pleasant, possibly, of whatever

19

nature, and my momentary way of experiencing that was to imagine all that it couldn't be. Why am I being given this? What's the trick? Well, thinking asks, "What's the trick?"[1]

When Creeley speaks about this personal "way of experiencing," he is also speaking about his poetic sensibility: he called one of his first volumes *The Whip* because the title defined his mode of perception.[2] In the poems collected in *The Whip,* published by Scribner's as Part 1 of *For Love: Poems 1950–1960,*[3] the speaker camouflages his fears and confusions with cynicism and arrogance. In fact, Creeley's use of an aloof tone and world-weary posture to express a painful reality and, at the same time, to distance himself from it, dominates the poems of *For Love* as a whole.

The mask he assumes enables him to discuss, in a composed way, anxieties that all but overwhelm him. He is preoccupied in this volume with tensions caused by his marriage, divorce, and remarriage. The poems of Part 1, written between 1950 and 1955, deal chiefly with Creeley's thoughts and feelings leading to the collapse of his first marriage. The poems of Part 2 were written in response to the dislocating separation and to the painful divorce in 1956. By the time Creeley wrote the poems of Part 3, he had remarried. Thus the collection catches the poet in the delicate circumstance of transferring his affection from one woman to another, all the while asking, "What's the trick?" But later poems also show him beginning to drop the mask, beginning to express his hopes and his fears about love in a more straightforward fashion.

Although the central issue in this volume—his relationship with his first wife—commands the foreground, a minor theme—Creeley's interest in poets who have influenced him and in his own commitment to poetry—deserves attention as well. His "way of experiencing" poetry by poets he claims to admire is closely related to his "way of experiencing" love. He seems compelled to take nothing for granted about his response to their work. For instance, he owes a great deal to Charles Olson, Ezra Pound, and William Carlos Williams for the example of their published work as well as for their private tutelage and encouragement; yet he willfully offers his opinion about their accomplishments. Creeley openly debates them even in his early poems where the influence is most evident. The result is that his tributes to other writers often turn out to be critical estimations of their poetic achievement. But in the later poems about poetry in the volume Creeley is more concerned with his own creative experience, both the satisfactions and the frustrations of the process. And, too, he begins to consider his fascination with words in terms of his need to feel independent: "That words, you can carry in your head and they're free. You don't need any particular materials other than the most minimal. . . . even if you don't have something to write on, you can possibly induce your memory to retain it."[4]

Creeley's attempt to analyze his interest in poetry has much in common with his attempt to scrutinize his relationship with women. In the last poems of *For Love*, he focuses attention on "conscious consciousness" itself. He wonders about the value of the posture he has exploited in the early poems, a detached posture designed to protect him from confronting the limiting contingencies of life head on.

FOR LOVE, PART 1

It seems Creeley arranged the first three poems in *For Love* with Valéry's discrimination in mind: among poetic monuments there are those which are mute or muffled, those which speak, and those which sing.[5] The fine opening poem of this volume deals with Hart Crane's "failed" poetic voice. "Hart Crane" begins with synaethesia—interchanging one sense for another—a technique associated with Crane:

> He had been stuttering, by the edge
> of the street, one foot still
> on the sidewalk, and the other
> in the gutter . . .
>
> like a bird, say, wired to flight, the
> wings, pinned to their motion, stuffed.
>   (p. 15)[6]

Creeley's brief portrait of Crane is an unkind one however accurate it may be. It would be hard to guess from the disturbing sense, casually put, or from the see-saw sound of the phrases mocking Crane's alcoholic stumbling, or from the image of a dead bird appropriately mounted by wire and pins, that Creeley actually admired

Crane's work. Later in the poem "Hart Crane," Creeley quotes
from "The Broken Tower," a poem in which Crane speaks about
his uncreative labors but, inspired by the alternating music of the
bells, gradually becomes more confident about his poetic powers.
In Creeley's poem, by contrast, the sing-song rhythm signals
futility. It is also ironic that one of the main points Creeley makes
in "Hart Crane and the Private Judgment" and "The Letters of
Hart Crane"[7] is that the publicized scandals in Crane's life and the
failure of the machine-age vision as developed in *The Bridge* too
often block a genuine appreciation of Crane's mastery of rhythm.
Creeley's poem does not follow the line of reasoning he sympathetically explored in the critical notes written years later. Rather, the
poem exploits Crane's homosexuality—"(Slater, let me come
home"—and his confusions—"But my own ineptness/ cannot bring
them [Slater Brown's words] to hand"—at the same time that the
poem demonstrates Creeley's impressive handling of consonantal
melodies.

Still more surprising than the patronizing tribute to Crane is the
second poem, "Le Fou," dedicated to Charles Olson. The gist of
"Le Fou" is that Olson plots the lines of the poem in an attempt to
register his breathing. The poem speaks of him as a plodding
innovator for whom, quite understandably, "graces come slowly,"
and pays him what could technically be called a compliment. Yet
the effect Olson hoped to achieve overall was one of driving
intensity: "ONE PERCEPTION MUST IMMEDIATELY AND
DIRECTLY LEAD TO A FURTHER PERCEPTION. . . . USE
USE USE the process at all points, in any given poem always,
always one perception must must must MOVE, INSTANTER, ON
ANOTHER!"[8] It is not that Creeley failed to distinguish between
Olson's major importance as a theorist and his moderate importance as a poet; rather, it is that Creeley indiscreetly calls attention
to the difference by repeatedly associating Olson with all that is
"slow."

Le Fou
for Charles

who plots, then, the lines
talking, taking, always the beat from
the breath
      (moving slowly at first

```
the breath
            which is slow—

I mean, graces come slowly,
it is that way.

So slowly (they are waving
we are moving
                  away from     (the trees
                      the usual    (go by
which is slower than this, is
                      (we are moving!
goodbye
```
                              (p. 17)

"Le Fou" is a transitional poem. "We are moving" from "Hart Crane" to "A Song," in which Creeley gives his own poetic achievement a privileged position and, within the organizational context, whether we know Valéry or not, a promising title.

In "A Song," Creeley brings together his major and minor themes: his feelings about Ann, his first wife, have serious repercussions apropos his creative spirit. First he describes the kind of poem he values and would like to make. Then he goes on to complain that because of his relationship with Ann, his poetic voice has been compromised and perhaps will be lost altogether.

A Song
for Ann

```
I had wanted a quiet testament
and I had wanted, among other things,
a song.
        That was to be
of a like monotony.
                      (A grace

Simply. Very very quiet.


                      A murmur of some lost
thrush, though I have never seen one.

Which was you then. Sitting
and so, at peace, so very much now this same quiet.
```

A song.

And of you the sign now, surely, of a gross
perpetuity
            (which is not reluctant, or if it is,
it is no longer important.

A song.

Which one sings, if he sings it,
with care.

                                        (p. 18)

In a tranquil moment, the speaker remembers what he "had
wanted." The possibility of his life and the possibility of his art
depended on Ann. She was the source and the embodiment of his
inspiration. He was to bear witness to his experience quietly and
simply. His song was to be unobtrusive yet special like "(A grace"
and compelling like "A murmur of some lost/ thrush." His feeling
for Ann was to be love "at peace." Within the context of poetic
association, the "testament," "song," and "you" become symbiotic
equivalents which shape and define each other.

     The second half of the poem begins on line 13, where the tense
shifts from past to present. Now the woman is "no longer" like the
unseen "lost/ thrush." Instead, she is "the sign now, surely, of a
gross/ perpetuity." Whether Creeley is referring to Ann's trust
fund or to her pregnancy ("gross/ perpetuity"), the point is that he
"no longer" feels inextricably bound up with her life. Although she
assures him continuance, he can stand back and speculate dispassionately about her motivations. The distance between what he
"had wanted" and what he has is conveyed by the sense of the
words and suggested by the difference in the weight of their sounds
as well: "grace," "gross"; "never seen," "sign now"; "a quiet
testament," "a gross perpetuity." Most crucial of all, he "no
longer" cares about her.

     "A song" must be made "with care"; yet he is distracted. The
creation of a "very very quiet" poem remains a possibility, but for
someone else. Ann has failed him. The kind of love, like the kind of
life and the kind of poem he "had wanted," are fragile memories.
Of course Creeley has given us the "song" he valued in the first
twelve lines of the poem. But the implication is that he cannot go

on in a graceful, murmuring way given the personal frustrations and disappointments he has to deal with.

Creeley's poetic universe is an intensely personal one in which the poet himself is the central figure. As "A Song" suggests, his life was filled with strains and stresses he was unable to manage. If half the stories about his fighting and drinking are true,[9] his behavior during the late forties and early fifties particularly can only be called frenetic: "I used to fight in just sheer frustration, and a feeling of absolute incompetence and inability."[10] There is an almost violent self-assertiveness just beneath the surface of Creeley's "very very quiet" early poems which project a humble posture. From time to time arrogance breaks through in a word or phrase as in "The Conspiracy" (p. 37): "Let us suddenly/ proclaim spring. And jeer// at the others/ all the others." Or perhaps a short poem's development takes an unexpected turn to expose the angry poet behind his mask. For instance, "The Crisis" (p. 19) begins meekly: "Let us say (in anger) that since the day we were married" and ends unpredictably with a damning comment about "rancor." Much of Creeley's low-keyed poetry springs from a serious sense of unswerving attention and a carefully guarded perspective such as we find in "The Innocence" (p. 24): "What I come to do/ is partial, partially kept."

Creeley is looking for a personal attitude which, once discovered and assumed, will allow him to take the world on his own terms. Or, to put it another way, his essentially self-centered poems record his attempt to maintain a sense of self-worth in the face of often threatening realities. In "The Dishonest Mailmen," the poet's cool, passive response to explicit hostility is a prelude to defiance (in the tradition of Eva Tanquay):

The Dishonest Mailmen

They are taking all my letters, and they
put them into a fire.

                              I see the flames, etc.
But do not care, etc.

They burn everything I have, or what little
I have. I don't care, etc.

The poem supreme, addressed to
emptiness—this is the courage

> necessary. This is something
> quite different.
>
> (p. 29)

We don't know why Creeley's letters arouse such outrage, and we
don't know if he has "the courage// necessary" to continue writing
them. The time lapse between "courage" and "necessary" suggests
that he may not. We do know he feels isolated with his purpose.
Gottfried Benn's[11] idea of the absolute poem ("The poem without
hope, the poem addressed to no one . . ."), which in "The
Dishonest Mailmen" is called "the poem supreme," gives the
speaker a chance to recover a serious artist's composure. But it is a
superficial gain. After all, there is no real difference in the poem
between "letters" destined for the "fire" and "The poem supreme,
addressed to/ emptiness."

What the poet seems to need is the ultimate in self-motivation or
at least a philosophical perspective and a sophisticated way of
saying, "I don't care, etc." A detached posture, articulately defined
and hopefully believed, is indeed "something quite different."
Creeley found a self-possessed yet passionately critical viewpoint in
Paul Valéry's *Monsieur Teste* and, as he told me:

> Teste's posture is something I much admired and really
> hungered in ways not to equal but to relate to; that is, to be in
> some ways parallel to. Valéry was fascinating to me as a
> writer, *Monsieur Teste* in particular. I still have a small
> clipping of a picture of him in his full academic dress. I really
> loved the handsomeness and tone of him.[12]

Creeley's admiration for Valéry and, specifically, his fascination
with *Monsieur Teste*, is evident in his poem "The Riddle." In this
poem, Creeley presents a sexual experience involving an "imperative" woman and a "man/ lost in stern/ thought" who meet "at the
edge of/ conception." The poem is a riddle because Creeley
describes their meeting in statements which seem unrelated to
each other and unrelated to the experience as a whole. Yet the poet
speaks with such assurance about what is happening that he
manages to engage our attention and challenge our ingenuity. Once
we recognize that the material in the poem is arranged according
to Teste's art of impersonal love, the puzzle can be solved.
Madame Emile Teste's account of making love with her "stern"

husband not only gives us the clues we need to crack the riddle but shows us the extent to which Creeley uses Teste's "system" in several of these early poems. First here is Creeley:

The Riddle

What it is, the literal size
incorporates.
            The question
is a mute question. One is
too lonely, one wants
to stop there, at the edge of

conception. The woman

imperative, the man
lost in stern
thought:

give it form certainly,
the names and titles.
           (p. 21)

And here is Madame Teste:

> That supreme certainty must arise out of a supreme uncertainty, and show itself to be the climax of a kind of drama whose pace and development we should find it difficult to trace, from calm up to the extreme threat of the event. . . . But Sir, when he comes back to me from the depths! . . . when this extraordinary husband takes hold and masters me, as it were, putting the imprint of his strength upon me, I feel that I am a substitute for some object of his will that just then escaped him. I am like the plaything of a muscular thought—I express it as best I can.[13]

Whereas Madame Teste describes the "drama," Creeley tries to reenact it by bringing us into the speaker's mind. We are to follow the protagonist into the "depths" and "come back" with him; we are to accept "the woman" as "a substitute for some object of his will that just then escaped him"; and we are to regard the poem at hand as justification for the energy he has expended.

    The speaker of "The Riddle" begins with a flat, contained statement of fact: "What it is, the literal size/ incorporates," and gives himself time to reflect calmly on it. There are countless possibilities but precisely what "it" refers to apparently does not matter. And we do not know how the second observation (lines 3–4) relates to the first. (Teste's insights were connected "by leaps that were no surprise to him.") Yet we are made to feel that the speaker, absorbed and alone, does know what is going on by the very decisiveness with which he offers his puzzling comment: "The question/ is a mute question." Some unspecified "particular" commands his attention, and as he pursues it, he becomes more excited. The syntax of the poem makes that clear.

The words—"at the edge of// conception"—place the speaker within range of that most-sought-most-unsought moment by their literal sense. But the period following the dramatic pause—"of// conception"—signals the end of the poet's intellectual activity; the moment remains elusive after all. "The woman," by following "conception" in line 7, is, as Madame Teste puts it, a "substitute." "The *knowing-knowledge* moment" never does materialize in "The Riddle." Nonetheless, the poet is "lost in stern/ thought"; and that state, according to Teste's "system of self-awareness," is most essential and, under these circumstances involving "the woman// imperative," most expected:

> T. In the very midst of love, Teste is pierced by his demon—knowledge.
>
> He perceives ideas through sensations of "pleasure." He feels another's orgasm, and that other, by a demonstration difficult to reproduce, *equates* Him and Self. . . .[14]

Creeley reproduces the drama—"from calm up to the extreme threat of the event"—through the sentence structure. He begins with a flat statement, refers to the question, and then moves to a disjointed run-on sentence. The intellectual drama does not climax with the imperative but with the command: "give it form certainly,/ the names and titles." Through the poem, the poet can *"equate* Him and Self" albeit his conclusion is tentative. The speaker has privately achieved a "provisional" thought. Whether he has achieved "that supreme certainty," to use the words of Madame Teste, is for "the woman" of "The Riddle" to say. The poem itself focuses on the intellectual drama rather than on the sexual experience.

Again in "The Business," the speaker distances himself from an emotionally charged situation. In this poem he celebrates feeling as an impersonal force he can use to advantage.

The Business

To be in love is like going outside to see what kind of day

it is. Do not
mistake me. If you love

her how prove she
loves also, except that it

occurs, a remote chance on
which you stake

yourself? But barter for
the Indian was a means of sustenance.

There are records.

(p. 44)

The opening simile expresses the poet's indifference to love, an indifference perhaps cultivated in response to love's uncertainty. He is either "the Indian" (the odd syntax "how prove she" in line 5 and the play on "stake" in line 8 suggest he is) or he is not. In any case, his hope that sex or love itself will "occur" is "a remote chance," far removed from his understanding that "barter for/ the Indian was a means of sustenance." Flippantly resigned to a tenuous relationship, to getting "The Business," the protagonist seems half-amused by his problems as his wry tone suggests. But then he can afford to be because he has made a poem of his unsettled feelings; he has made a "record."

Whether or not Creeley set out to rewrite *Monsieur Teste* is not the point; rather, it is that Creeley's cynical posture toward women in these early poems has much in common with Valéry's. A comparison between Creeley's tone and vocabulary in "The Business" and Valéry's tone and vocabulary in "Anatecta" and "Suite" is to the point as well. Valéry refused to allow the external manifestations of emotion to enter his poetic universe; but he made one exception. He was interested in "a purified, 'dry' emotion" and, as he says in "Anatecta," it is the poet's "business" to produce one.[15] Creeley begins "The Business" by characterizing the speaker as sufficiently contemptuous of his feelings that we might expect him to follow this directive. Keeping in mind that for Valéry emotion was a defect in man's nature, consider this early passage from "Suite" as the source of Creeley's characterization of the speaker in "The Business":

> The man incredulous as to his feelings, and without illusion as to his SELF who would watch himself blush as he would watch a reagent color a solution—this sage—will therefore have to endure his life like a strange necessity—love, suffer, endure, desire—as one greets the days and the fluctuations of the weather.[16]

In the midsection of "The Business," the speaker explains that "barter" is the condition of the sexual relationship between him and the woman, an analogy Valéry often uses to justify the investment of emotion. The most profitable such investment, as Valéry says in this late passage from "Suite," has to do with love:

> The true (that is, usable) value of love is in the increase of general vitality which it may afford.
> Any love that does not release this energy is bad.
> The procedure is to utilize this sexual ferment for other purposes. What assumed it had only men to make is employed to produce acts, works.[17]

The final lines of "The Business"—"But barter for/ the Indian was a means of sustenance.// There are records."—bring with them the sexual connotations bound up with "stake." The poem as a whole makes use of, "utilizes," a tenuous sexual relationship. Although Creeley does not say explicitly the "value of love" is that it provides "sexual ferment" which in turn can be "employed" by the artist to "produce acts, words," perhaps the fullest interpretation of "The Business" turns on Valéry's assumption.

In "The Immoral Proposition," Creeley plays off the lure of the dispassionate, speculative stance against what is felt to be a mandate for active participation. The argument turns on the opening word:

The Immoral Proposition

If you never do anything for anyone else
you are spared the tragedy of human relation-

ships. If quietly and like another time
there is the passage of an unexpected thing:

to look at it is more
than it was. God knows

nothing is competent nothing is
all there is. The unsure

egoist is not
good for himself.

(p. 31)

Creeley's central theme is "human relation-// ships." The effect of
breaking up "relation-// ships" in his poem is to focus attention on
"ships," which, like relationships, move in often unanticipated
ways: "there is the passage of an unexpected thing." A "tragic"
relationship that comes to "nothing" has its own dynamics and that
in itself can become the impetus for creative activity: "to look at it
is more/ than it was." What the poet seems to need is the
confidence to follow where the relationship leads. Lacking it ("The
unsure// egoist is not/ good for himself"), Creeley protects his
vulnerability by retreating into the Monsieur Teste posture, a
stance that enables him to withdraw from the world and emerge
seemingly superior to it.

The conflict implied between the detached intelligence brooding
on its own intricacies and the all-inclusive human response facing
squarely the painful contingencies of life is most obvious when
Creeley's subject is women. His most interesting poems about
women make use of Monsieur Teste's pose; but there are several
fine poems in this collection which make use of more conventional
attitudes. "The Whip," for instance, deals with a restless husband,
his unresponsive wife, and his almost satisfying fantasy involving
"another woman":

The Whip

I spent a night turning in bed,
my love was a feather, a flat

sleeping thing. She was
very white

and quiet, and above us on
the roof, there was another woman I

also loved, had
addressed myself to in

a fit she
returned. That

encompasses it. But now I was
lonely, I yelled,

but what is that? Ugh,
she said, beside me, she put

her hand on
my back, for which act

I think to say this
wrongly.

(p. 51)

The poem begins with a stimulating promise: "I spent the night turning in bed." But of the countless appositional phrases which might describe "my love was a feather," the anticlimatic phrase, "a flat// sleeping thing," is at least among the most disappointing. In an effort to account for the distance between the stimulating promise and the disappointing reality, Robert Duncan, in his brief review of *For Love*, refers to this poem and comments: "But for Creeley what is held in the mind is to be realized in the act, and poetry arises in the constant working of tangible substance and idea." He goes on to describe the "cause and effect" of this poem as "a synthesis of a moral demand and an esthetic demand."[18] Duncan does not analyze the dynamics of this "synthesis" but he does cite the dramatic core of the poem:

> . . . above us on
> the roof, there was another woman I
>
> also loved, had
> addressed myself to in

a fit she
returned. That

encompasses it . . .

We can "hear" the speaker's sexual excitement mount as the
back and front vowel sounds alternate in increasingly rapid suc-
cession, climax on the long *e* rhyme—"she/ returned"—and then
relax physically but not emotionally: "That// encompasses it. But
now I was lonely." It is not clear, however, which "act" the
speaker regrets. Was he wrong to "love" the imagined woman or
wrong to care about the woman sleeping beside him who perhaps
wields the whip and somehow compels the poem? "I think to say
this/ wrongly" calls the speaker's poetic voice into question—its
character as well as its purpose. The ambiguous syntax in the last
lines of the poem reflects the speaker's general state of confusion
and unhappiness. Yet "wrongly" echoes "lonely," suggesting that
the guilt-burdened speaker's chief complaint is self-directed; it is
wrong for him to be in a lonely relationship, to think about it, and
to speak about it.

Creeley often focuses on a recognizable woman in his early
poems and then, following Stendhal in *On Love*, "weaves a
collection of strange fantasies" around her.[19] Or, to use Duncan's
judgment, "the Lady is both archetypical and specific" in *For
Love*.[20] Creeley's hope, perhaps, is that the characterization will
hold on both levels, the domestic and the imaginary, with the result
that the poem will be complex and provocative rather than merely
confessional. What we often get, however, is a personal poem in
which the woman is not credible in human terms or in "archetypical" terms. "A Form of Adaptation," "The Operation," "The
Rhyme," and "The Disappointment" present women who are too
strange to be part of commonly shared experience but who are too
ordinary to be fantastic. As Creeley's poetic voice matures, he will
say in the poem itself that an experience with his wife leads him to
think about women in general; or he will set a "combination"
woman within an explicitly drug-induced atmosphere where concrete, palpable reality and transcendent wisdoms meet, as in "The
Finger" from *Pieces*. By contrast, from the very beginning of his
career, Creeley was able to deal with male friendship in straightforward terms. For instance, there is this unmistakable sense of
openness in Creeley's poems that project thoughts and feelings

about friends, as in "For Rainer Gerhardt,"[21] but only in his most recent sequence, "In London," does he "receive" women as friends and treat them with the directness heretofore reserved for men. Creeley's major theme has to do with the give and take of human relationships. Whether his poems record his candid perceptions or his self-conscious, ulterior motives is the problem.

Conclusions and questions, then, emerge from a study of the poems in *For Love*, Part 1. Creeley's sharpened consciousness is his subject; his own mind is at the center and at the circumference of the poem. His poetic posture, the nature of the mask through which he filters his thoughts and feelings, is the issue. The poems which concern women, such as "A Song," "The Riddle," and "The Business," are basically poignant expressions although they are superficially cynical ones. Creeley's ironic characterization of a love imagined as a transactionary gain owes a great deal to Valéry's portrayal of Monsieur Teste, who considered marriage a bargain in the sense of human exchange. Yet, as his poems attest, Creeley tried to salvage his marriage and was deeply unhappy when it collapsed. It is useless to argue whether his detached attitude toward women was cultivated in self-defense during an awkward time or whether his supercilious attitude toward women led to his divorce in the first place. The central point is that Creeley's early poems about love are filled with both calculated irony and genuine desperation.

There is a similar mixture of attitudes in the poems which concern poem making, Creeley's minor theme in this section. In "The Innocence" and in "The Dishonest Mailmen," he seems to cherish his insularity. Yet, at the same time, "The Innocence" is addressed to the reader—"What I come to do/ is partial, partially kept"—and "The Dishonest Mailmen" is not "addressed to/ emptiness—" but is in fact "something/ quite different." The poems dedicated to other poets, namely "Hart Crane" and "Le Fou," present contradictory messages as well. On the one hand, he suggests his admiration for Crane and Olson; on the other hand, he defines himself as their competitor.

FOR LOVE, PART 2

Creeley wrote most of the poems of Part 2 in response to the

disordering collapse of his first marriage. Taken together, these
self-analytic poems evidence his need to sort the confusions.
Creeley finds there is nothing outside himself he can really depend
on. It is not that he rejects everything and everyone but that he
comes to realize he is essentially on his own. "The Flower," the
most memorable lyric in Part 2, conveys that sense of seemingly
endless, all-pervasive emotional pain which temporarily qualifies
Creeley's smug posture in his earlier poetry:

> The Flower
>
> I think I grow tensions
> like flowers
> in a wood where
> nobody goes.
>
> Each wound is perfect,
> encloses itself in a tiny
> imperceptible blossom,
> making pain.
>
> Pain is a flower like that one,
> like this one,
> like that one,
> like this one.
>
> (p. 96)

The poet's meditation takes place in an isolated wood, a personalized place of self-consciousness. Each flower embodies his pain
and, by growing, naturally adds to his burden. The poem pits the
lonely victim's endurance against his vulnerability and, in the final
stanza, suggests his capacity to sustain exquisite misery, perfect in
its completeness and intensity. Although the last lines do not find
him counting buttons on a hangman's coat as Monsieur Teste
would, they do testify to his verbal stamina in the face of anxiety
which executes itself and perpetuates itself with artless delicacy, as
represented by the flower. At the same time, the evil flower, in the
tradition of Baudelaire, corresponds to his "inward life," and John
Constable's description of Creeley's best poems in *For Love* is
relevant here:

> Creeley's best poems inhabit that area of tension between the
> inward life of an individual and the outward world of objects,

the 'inner and outer weather' of Frost's famous poem. . . . or the design suggested by Pound, a recording of 'the precise instant when a thing outward and objective transforms itself, or darts into a thing inward and subjective.' "[22]

In many poems in this section Creeley focuses on "that area of tension between the inward life of an individual and the outward world of objects." He measures "outward" expectation against personally experienced actuality in an effort to explain to himself, and incidentally to us, what went wrong with his marriage. One way to follow his thinking and feeling is to follow his attitude toward "form," a key word in Part 2. In "The Letter," the poet makes the distinction between marriage as an "inward," personal occasion and marriage as an "outward" form:

> . . . I thought the pain was endless
> but the form existent,
> as it is form
> and as such I loved it . . .
>
> (p. 97)

He comes to a more instructive moment of self-awareness in "The Place." The speaker discovers that "the form" is "the gro-/ tesquerie—" because it intervenes between the literal reality and his understanding of it. Sorting out the confusions is a complicated business, and the poem is faithful to the complexity of intellect-ually arguing that the event per se defines the significant form:

The Place

What is the form is the gro-
tesquerie—the accident
of the moon's light
on your face.

Oh love, an empty table!
An empty bottle also.
But no trick will go
so far but not further.

The end of the year is a division, a drunken derision
of composition's accident.
We both fell.

I fell. You fell.
In hell we will tell of it.
Form's accidents, we move back-
wards to love . . .

The movement of the
sentence tells me of you
as it was the bottle we drank?
No. It was no accident.

Agh, form is what happens?
Form is an accompaniment.
I to love, you to love:
syntactic accident.

It will all come true,
in a year.
The empty bottle, the empty table,
tell where we were.

(p. 98)

It is all here: the insult, the philosophical sigh, the guarded hint at
reconciliation, the professionally framed explanation, and the
prediction of finality in straightforward lines to which the speaker
entrusts his composure. The important point is that marriage as a
"form" loses its value as the poem progresses. "The empty bottle,
the empty table" replace "form's accidents" as measures of "what
happens." In "The Hill," the last poem of Part 2, Creeley says:

But that form, I must answer
is dead in me, completely,
and I will not allow it
to reappear—

(p. 104)

This brave passage foreshadows these crucial lines from *Pieces* (p.
68): "Want to get the sense of 'I' into Zukofsky's 'eye'—a/ locus of
experience, not a presumption of expected value."

Another way to follow Creeley's growing insistence that we must
substitute personal response, however awkward, for inherited
formulations, however sophisticated, is to look at those poems in
which he appeals to his wife to reconsider their relationship.
"Ballad of the Despairing Husband" is a parody of the "cult of

Amor," and "Air: 'Cat Bird Singing' " is a more graceful variation on the same theme. In them, Creeley alternately addresses the "Lady" and his wife. First consider the final stanzas of "Ballad of the Despairing Husband" and then "Air: 'Cat Bird Singing' ":

> Oh lovely lady, morning or evening or afternoon,
> Oh lovely lady, eating with or without a spoon.
> Oh most lovely lady, whether dressed or undressed or partly.
> Oh most lovely lady, getting up or going to bed or sitting only.
>
> Oh loveliest of ladies, than whom none is more fair, more
>   gracious, more beautiful.
> Oh loveliest of ladies, whether you are just or unjust,
>   merciful, indifferent, or cruel.
> Oh most loveliest of ladies, doing whatever, seeing
>   whatever, being whatever.
> Oh most loveliest of ladies, in rain, in shine, in
>   any weather.
>
> Oh lady, grant me time,
> please, to finish my rhyme.
>
> (from "Ballad of the Despairing Husband," p. 77)

Air: "Cat Bird Singing"

> Cat bird singing
> makes music like sounds coming
>
> at night. The trees, goddam them,
> are huge eyes. They
>
> watch, certainly, what
> else should they do? My love
>
> is a person of rare refinement,
> and when she speaks,
>
> there is another air,
> melody—what Campion spoke of
>
> with his
> follow thy faire sunne unhappie shadow . . .

> Catbird, catbird.
> O lady hear me. I have no
>
> other
> voice left.
>
> (p. 69)

Duncan says the "Lady" of both poems "is a power in women that Dante once knew in Beatrice and that, before Dante, troubadours of Provence addressed in their love songs and petitions."[23] If Duncan's insights are to be helpful to us, a more emphatic distinction must be made between the "power in women" and the "Lady" herself. These poems about love may well be poignant pleas to the "power in women." But Creeley's addresses to the "Lady" are devoid of humility and reverence. He uses the troubadours' "love songs and petitions" in "Ballad of the Despairing Husband" and Thomas Campion's song in "Air: 'Cat Bird Singing' " to establish traditional contexts in which to register his unhappiness. At the same time, the satiric tone in "Ballad of the Despairing Husband" and the shifting diction in "Air: 'Cat Bird Singing' " suggest that Creeley will stick by his own insights and his own words.

Challenging the authority of established conventions, Creeley uses satire and self-parody in these two poems, thereby personalizing the forms so that they become relevant vehicles for his own expression. Perhaps the judgment that Creeley is challenging authority overstates the case; nonetheless, the feeling that Creeley deems modification to be in order is inescapable. Here, as in several poems in Part I in which he wrote with qualified admiration about poets he respects, he offers his critical comment. For instance, in "Heroes," he speaks about "Virgil's plan . . . that it was of course human enough to die,/ yet to come back," and goes on to say: "That was the Cumaean Sibyl speaking./ This is Robert Creeley." The idea that the speaker's individualized response is the crucial one is underscored by "Going to Bed," the poem which follows "Heroes." In "Going to Bed," Creeley gives us his own version of "it was of course human enough to die,/ yet to come back":

> It is a viscous form of self-
> propulsion that lets the feet grip
> the floor, as the head
> lifts to the door,

lurches, ghostwise, out, and to
the window to fall through,
yet closes it to let
the cat out too.

After that, silence, silence.
On the floor, the hands
find quiet, the mouth goes lax.
 · · · · · · · · · · · · · · · · .(p. 95)

Whereas "in all those stories the hero/ is beyond himself into the next/ thing" ("Heroes"), Creeley's speaker is more credibly stopped by the instinct for self-preservation. Like the Cumaean Sibyl, he survives (as reluctantly?) to write it down—*"hic opus, hic labor est."*

A sense of loneliness and bitterness mark the poems in this section. Although Warren Tallman's observation about Creeley's poetry is sound in general—

> There are many wrong ways to look at Robert Creeley's art but the wrongest is that which sees it flowing from an inner angst, emptiness or despair, as though he had come to believe that modern lives, his own included, are little more than, in Whitman's phrase, "a suck and a sell."[24]

—the poems of *For Love*, Part 2, do, in fact, flow from an "inner angst" and, taken together, they do make up an unusually depressing collection. Creeley has, of course, written about "emptiness" before and he will continue to do so; but never does he give us, as he does here, a poetic record of composite personal experience in which "inner angst, emptiness or despair" dominates, actually threatens to overwhelm, his viewpoint. He is more typically, as Tallman says, a "tough customer," a "conspicuous instance of full-bodied resistance to despair."[25] "The Invoice" serves to measure the darkness of Creeley's mood in Part 2. Of all his poems throughout the volumes which deal with the friendship motif, this one alone registers disappointment unmitigated by affection or admiration:

The Invoice

I once wrote a letter as follows:
dear Jim, I would like to borrow
200 dollars from you
to see me through.

> I also wrote another: dearest M/
> please come.
> There is no one
> here at all.
>
> I got word today,
> viz: hey
> sport, how are you making it?
> And, why don't you get with it.
>   (p. 86)

The sense of urgency born by long suffering is intensified by Creeley's ironic use of colloquial speech, glibly put. This kind of diction, like the informal language in the often anthologized distressing poem "I Know a Man," seems merely to report (in vernacular already dated) the speaker's direct perception of the moment, unprocessed, unheightened, unshaped by any device which might transform its raw personal content into a self-transcendent "literary" experience. "The Invoice" recognizes the integrity, hence the aesthetic purpose, of its improvisational tone. In *Words*, a volume given over to the exploration and illustration of various definitions and modes of poetry, Creeley assesses the usefulness of this kind of poetic statement. The casually bitter, tossed-off quality of "The Invoice" closely resembles an effect Creeley says he wants, among others, in *Words*—an effect he achieves in the "here are unpolished fragments from my notebook" portions of *Pieces* and *A Day Book*. In those sequences, the speaker's lapse into matter-of-fact, seemingly spontaneous proselike poetry supports his credibility as a human being and relieves the tension created by his convoluted, intellectual forays. "The Invoice" is one of Creeley's earliest attempts to make use of the colloquial idiom.

In *For Love*, Part 2, Creeley tries through a variety of poetic moods and contexts to involve us in his argument with his wife. In fact, the most striking feature of this collection, apart from the speaker's unhappiness, is its variety. It is helpful in a study of Creeley's poetry to isolate those elements, both of form and of content, with which he will continue to work in his later poetry. First, the friendly, somewhat humorous, flexibly useful tone of "Oh No" emerges from the assortment of voices presented here (which range from the whine to the distinctly literate) to dominate his later volumes of poetry:

Oh No

If you wander far enough
you will come to it
and when you get there
they will give you a place to sit

for yourself only, in a nice chair,
and all your friends will be there
with smiles on their faces
and they will likewise all have places.[26]
(p. 62)

At his best, Creeley will break the casual mood abruptly with an intense line—angry, anguished, painfully sad—relying on the juxtaposition of tones to achieve the texture of an actively engaged, recognizably human voice. Second, when Creeley means to suggest the esoteric and magical, he does not establish the context of *romance* and proceed, as Jerome Mazzaro says, in "Dantean fashion" recalling the perilous journeys of depth psychology."[27] In "Ballad of the Despairing Husband" and "Air: 'Cat Bird Singing,'" to name two such "journeys," it is difficult to distinguish between Creeley's attitude toward the literary convention he uses and his attitude toward the actual subject of his poem. However, his updated substitutes—strange, drug-induced visions here represented by "A Wicker Basket"—are not always understandable either.

Third and most important, the "Lady" the burdened poet stumbles after in "The Door" and the equally abstract one he cannot touch in "A Form of Woman" disappear along with his silly, stylized, agonized response to them. So do the uncharacterized stock "particulars" of "A Marriage" and "Sing Song," women who elicit his self-pitying, coyly put reactions. The woman the fearful, hopeful poet addresses in the aesthetically and psychologically satisfying "If You" is the one he keeps on talking to in the coming volumes, though his tone will soften.

If You

If you were going to get a pet
what kind of animal would you get.

A soft bodied dog, a hen—
feathers and fur to begin it again.

When the sun goes down and it gets dark
I saw an animal in a park

Bring it home, to give it to you.
I have seen animals break in two.

You were hoping for something soft
and loyal and clean and wondrously careful—

a form of otherwise vicious habit
can have long ears and be called a rabbit.

Dead. Died. Will die. Want.
Morning, midnight. I asked you

if you were going to get a pet
what kind of animal would you get.

(p. 79)

We learn just enough about the woman, who compelled the poet's response and who perpetuates it by her silence, to recognize and grasp her actual presence. And, too, we learn just enough about the poet to realize that he is finding it increasingly difficult to disassociate himself from human relations. Within the stabilizing framework of rhymed couplets, the speaker's cool, flippant sarcasm is checked by rhythmic and syntactic disruptions until stanza 7, where the general pattern breaks down altogether, exposing his almost speechless determination to continue hoping and continue asking. The poem's interplay of similar sounds stays in the mind to suggest we take the concluding stanza as the first and begin with the speaker the presumably endless process again. (As in "The Flower," sheer endurance offers more promise and, by implication, more comfort than change.)

Creeley seemed to relish his almost self-destructive habit of relating to insistent, unforgiving women he could barely cope with, as this comment from his brief critical note on William Carlos Williams suggests:

We can hope that the woman be merciful, a kind of repose (and our rejection in part) for that for which she attacks. And yet there is no woman either to be kind or to live with a kind man, and rightly. The man who would come to her comes with his own weapons, and if he is not a fool, he uses them.[28]

As the poems in Part 2 make plain, Creeley's arsenal includes the Monsieur Teste affectation, the "archetypical Lady" fantasy, and the wife as stereotype. As he and his poetic voice mature, he will give up the detached perspective and deal with his feelings about women in a more straightforward fashion.

FOR LOVE, PART 3

Creeley continues to be preoccupied with love and marriage in the poems of Part 3. Most of the poems in this section record the speaker's confusions and hopes as he first considers and then tentatively accepts the possibility of love again. The theme does not dominate these poems, written between 1959 and 1960, to the extent that it dominated Part 2. There is room in Part 3 for "pure" meditative poems in which the speaker focuses attention on the act of thinking. And, too, there is room for poems about the jest, the glory, and the riddle of poem making, a theme lost in the tangle of personal self-castigations, self-explanations, and self-assurances of Part 2.

"The Figures," while demonstrating Creeley's possession of lyrical genius beyond quarrel, gives evidence of his serious concern with poem making itself. The poem presents an erotic experience involving the artist and his medium. It is finally a more sophisticated and a more authentically realized erotic circumstance than the one conveyed by the much admired "Kore," which achieves its sensual effect from the obviously suggestive, myth-inspired scene the poet observes: "a lady/ accompanied/ by goat men/ leading her." In "The Figures," Creeley focuses meditative attention on the creative process, "the act of making." He notes the artist's complete, loving surrender to his material, the singularity and mute permanence of the autonomous finished product and, with slightly less certainty, the maker's exquisite satisfaction:

> The Figures
> The stillness
> of the wood,
> the figures formed
>
> by hands so still
> they touched it
> to be one

hand holding one
hand, faces
without eyes

bodies of wooden
stone, so still
they will not move

from that quiet
action ever
again. Did the man

who made them find
a like quiet? In
the act of making them

it must have been
so still he heard the wood
and felt it with his hands

moving into
the forms
he has given to them,

one by singular
one, so quiet,
so still.

(p. 147)

The melodic line, shaped and controlled by "still" and "quiet" weaving through the stolid alliterations, moves insistently down the open stanzas to expose and define a paradoxically powerful yet fragile aesthetic area of poetic "forms" in which Creeley will examine (and reexamine in other poems) his own medium: words. The immediate sense of this poem relates to the sculptor's experience with his literally too good to be true material of "wooden/ stone," a material which is pliable yet fixable, if not beyond distortion then at least highly resistant to it. That "wooden/ stone" does not, in fact, exist checks the poet's implied wish to exchange words for wood and voice for hands in an effort to achieve a tactile, physical source material for his art. Though the artist is denied an ideal medium and a guarantee of complete satisfaction, there are, "The Figures" argues, aesthetic goals that can be attained. The maker can become totally immersed "In/ the act of making" so that his response to the material entirely fills the activity, crowding out the issue of personal gratification. "The figures formed," "so quiet,/ so still," are self-contained and self-sufficient; neither their meaning nor the artist's pleasure derived from the making depends on the nonmaker's response: "faces/without eyes" are ideally free to induce serenity or eerie discomfort.

"After Mallarmé" is another reference point in a study of Creeley's poetry on poetry for several reasons, not the least of which is its graceful beauty. In this "imitative," chiseled, cameo poem, Creeley affirms his faith in the power of his words to follow and reveal the mind's activity:

After Mallarmé

    Stone,
    like stillness,
    around you my
    mind sits, it is

    a proper form
    for
    it, like
    stone, like

    compression itself,
    fixed fast,
    grey,
    without a sound.
               (p. 152)

Total rest—"So quiet,/ so still"—is given as an aesthetic ideal. Taken literally, the bare language of the poem creates a silence "around you" concealing the poet's attitude and purpose. With arrogance or perhaps with love, but surely with an air of confidence, he finds "a proper form." That is, "After Mallarmé" concentrates its meaning in an image of silent power: "You" is completely isolated. Creeley's awesome capabilities, here self-announced and self-assured, are checked in "The People," the poem which follows in the text. Nonetheless, "After Mallarmé" defines an aesthetic alternative, one that assumes the reader's active attention and goes on to the more interesting idea of focusing on the substantiality of the words themselves. Yet despite

the example of Mallarmé, the poet-reader relationship becomes a
concern per se for Creeley in the sequences, a motif which can be
traced back to his early invitations to the reader to share in the
experience of the poem.

The seriousness of Creeley's overt attempt to elicit the reader's
response is disclosed rather than undermined by his use of
self-directed irony. Here in "A Token" the wistful speaker gently,
yet nervously, raises a question about the value of words. The
hesitant tone, created by the conspicuous terminal junctures in the
first stanza, gradually relaxes in the second stanza where the poet
defines his hope:

> A Token
> My lady
> fair with
> soft
> arms, what
>
> can I say to
> you—words, words
> as if all
> worlds were there.
>   (p. 123)

John Corrington, who writes "that Robert Creeley is one of the
most exorbitantly overrated poets practicing today," faults this
poem for its "banality of thought" and calls it "a transcendent
invitation to boredom." He also says that "A Token" is one of
several poems in Part 3 which share the platitudinous assumption
"that language must give way to a more pointed tool in the
presence of love."[29] His wit aside, surely Corrington has missed the
act of creation here. "Fair with/ soft/ arms" is a world, sensually
inviting and tinged with danger, especially if "fair" is taken in the
physical sense. Creeley would transpose the "world" into "words,
words" (a hope repeated in "The Gift" and "Air: The Love of a
Woman") in an attempt to win the lady's approval—an ambitious
attempt surely.

Yet "A Token" is not a pretentious poem because of the halting
rhythm of its brittle lines. Critics have noted Creeley's significant
use of irregular line breaks, and their judgments are relevant here.
Robert Duncan makes the connection between Creeley's method of

phrasing a "composition where the crisis of the form is everywhere immediate" and his reason for doing so:

> It is the fact that no pattern can be taken for granted as a given procedure but that every measure means decision, immediately carries the crux of the form, that demands the subtle feeling for measure, the accuracy and fine sense of proportion characteristic of Creeley's art.[30]

Richard Howard also concludes that the "question of broken form" is of "great importance to Creeley's work" because Creeley thinks of a poem as "something made to be—or to appear—fragmentary, partial, incomplete," a technique which serves to convey his basic attitude: "Only the broken surface reveals the truth."[31] In "A Token" the disjointed mode of address together with the self-mocking qualification, "as if," suggests the poet's dilemma. On the one hand, he might measure his identity as a poet against the value of his own impulses and aspirations; on the other hand, he might be forced to define his role in terms of what others decide his words can actually do.

Here Creeley deals with his hopes and fears about his poetry from a personal point of view as "A Token" illustrates. In contrast to the early poems found in Part 1, he no longer comments on the intentions and achievements of other poets. Nor does he blame his frustrations with words on his insensitive wife or on an unsympathetic public. Rather, he begins to reevaluate his commitment to poetry in terms of his own ability and his own goals. Similarly, Creeley faces squarely the difficulties involved in careful analytical thinking. In the poems about thinking in Part 3, Creeley does not hide his confusions behind a posture of indifference to the reader's attempt to understand as he did in his earlier poems. He focuses, instead, on his mind's exhilarating twists and, more often, contradictory turns as it pursues the unknowable from the point of view of one who wants to study his own mind's structure and operation but who finds that the project is beyond his capability. We get a fine illustration of his more candid manner in "For Love."

In *For Love's* title poem, dedicated to his second wife, Creeley tries to make a definitive statement about love. He attempts to gather his thoughts together as this hesitant sounding passage, full of the unsaid, suggests:

If the moon did not . . .
no, if you did not
I wouldn't either, but
what would I not

do, what prevention, what
thing so quickly stopped.
That is love yesterday
or tomorrow, not

now. . . .
            (p. 159)

He is determined to understand love because all he knows
"derives/ from what it teaches" him. Yet, he concludes, his
thoughts are "vague." He is unable to make a statement about love
which is both valid and useful to him. The central point is that he
takes responsibility for his failure.

Here is tedium,
despair, a painful
sense of isolation and
whimsical if pompous

self-regard. But that image
is only of the mind's
vague structure, vague to me
because it is my own.
            (pp. 159–60)

The poet, both victim and torturer (as he also presents himself in
"The Plan"), agonizes over the possibility that love might be
defined in such a way as to make its reality accessible and
malleable. Unable to realize his ambition, he gives up the pursuit:
"no/ mind left to// say anything at all." The final lines of "For
Love" show the poet resigned to not-knowing: "Into the company
of love/ it all returns."

Perhaps Creeley's inability to get at the definition of love
accounts for his decision to expand his "way of experiencing" by
including antithought as a sought-after possibility. The state of
mindless rest becomes an antidote for cerebral exhaustion which in
turn heightens the significance of complex thought by commenting

on the toll it takes. In several poems in Part 3, Creeley directs our attention to his need to achieve the self-discipline necessary to stop thinking, literally. In "The Rain" he is "locked" in conscious consciousness: "What am I to myself/ that must be remembered,/ insisted upon/ so often?" and he wants to escape from the intellectual struggle through sexual love. In "Out of Sight," the poet's "eye shuts/ as a fist/ to hold patience,/ patience,/ in the locked mind" and he tries to escape "with face// of a clown." In "The End of the Day," the speaker caressingly welcomes sleep—

> . . . Night,
>
> good and sweet
> night, good
> night, good, good,
> night, has come.
>   (p. 135)

—to counter despair. Creeley uses the passive, nonthinking state to measure the intensity of his complicated intellectualizing. He makes his need for antithought psychologically convincing by relating it to various emotional and mental drains occasioned by day-to-day experience.

Although the nature of the intellectual process becomes an important theme, Creeley takes his primary sense of the world from the play of relationships, a drama in which he is the main character. In Part 3 of *For Love*, he is preoccupied with remarriage, an issue which makes it necessary for him to redefine his relationship with his first wife. In several poems ("The Memory," "Yellow," "To And," and "The People") Creeley attempts generously but decisively to relegate past mistakes to the past. "The First Time," a suspiciously calm recollection, is the finest of these backward glances:

> The First Time
>
> We are given a chance,
> among the worst something left
> otherwise, hopeful
> circumstance.

As I spoke to you,
once,
I loved you
as simply as that.

Now to go back,
I cannot
but going on,
will not forget the first time.

You likewise
with me must be
testament
to pain's indifference.

We are only careful
for such a memory, more
careful, I think,
than we ever thought to be.

(p. 146)

Conceivably, Creeley simply makes peace with a lost possibility;
yet the sincerity of his poem seems forced. Perhaps it is the shift
from "I" to "You likewise" to the even more complacent "We" or
perhaps it is the cool aloofness of the speaker's philosophizing
about "pain's indifference." Nonetheless, Creeley strikes a genuine
note in the last lines. If read with sympathy, "The First Time"
presents a subtle interplay of self-guarded condensation and utter
conviction. If read without it, "The First Time" presents the
necessary gesture, the presumptuous dissolution of emotion by
words, the "careful" affixing of pain to memory

The question of sincerity in this poem recalls Creeley's use of a
contrived mien in the poems about love in Part 1. "The Business,"
for instance, depended heavily on irony for its effect. Irony is less
obtrusive in "The First Time"; yet it is an important aspect of the
poem and as such it points up Creeley's awkwardness when the
issue is love. He also protects his vulnerability, when remarriage is
the debated subject, by characterizing himself as powerless to
make a decision. Commitment to another woman becomes a
matter of subconscious motivations and destined choices.

Of these essentially ambivalent poems ("Song," "The Rose," "The Gesture," and "The Wife," among them), "Love Comes Quietly" is the most memorable. This poem is a hesitantly framed reflection on marriage.

Love Comes Quietly

Love comes quietly
finally, drops
about me, on me,
in the old ways.

What did I know
thinking myself
able to go
alone all the way.
(p. 151)

The hesitant tone is created by the repetitive and the near repetitive sounds and constructions: "quietly" : "finally," "about me" : "on me," "in the old ways" : "alone all the way." Repetition gives the cautious poet time to catch the relevant feeling and find its verbal equivalent while we wait, and near repetition expresses his determination to qualify, however minutely, what he has already said. Creeley's conflicting impulses are dealt with in terms of opposing directional forces: "Love comes" : "myself/ able to go." It might be that he will break new territory in an unknown wilderness; or it might be that he will simply retrace an old path through a familiar landscape. Creeley asks himself a difficult question in this poem; he concludes that he does not know the answer. His problem is of special concern to the sympathetic reader because there is a sense of sequence about the poems in *For Love*, which begins with "A Song" for Ann and ends with "For Love" for Bobbie, that heightens the effect of the latest poems in the volume, such as "Love Comes Quietly."

In summary, much of the tension in Creeley's poems in *For Love* that deal with marriage—the central theme—and poetry and thinking—the minor themes—comes from the implied contradiction between his intelligence and his intuition. On the one hand, he is determined to explore moments of his own experience analytically; on the other, he senses that the exercise of his intelligence would not bring him to discover anything he could use in a meaningfully systematic way. In an interview with Lewis MacAdams, Creeley made the connection between his fascination with thinking, as well as his faith in its power, and the seminal attitude he held when these poems were written: "mind was thought of as the primary agent of having place in the world." He said that during the sixties he began to realize that he "wanted to get out of that awful assumption that thinking is the world,"[32] an assumption central to the Monsieur Teste sensibility. In retrospect, Creeley recognized the artificiality of believing in

> that duality that absolutely informs all my thinking as when I'm a kid, for example, that, you know, "the mind is to discipline the body," or "the body is to relax the mind." "You get drunk in order to relax your thinking. You think in order not to get drunk." It's a weird tension and the torque that's created by that systematization of experience is just awful.[33]

What was implict in *For Love*—the problems generated by Creeley's separation of intelligence and intuition, mind and body, thinking and sensory perception—becomes an explicit issue in *Words*.

2

WORDS

"I conclude from this that
we're all alike in our pro-
fession: we're all galley-
slaves, we're all tattooed."
    —Jean-Paul Sartre, *The Words*

The poems in *Words* show Robert Creeley looking for a way to measure his accomplishment in the world. His early poems, collected in *For Love*, attest to the fact that he once defined himself in terms of the power of his intelligence, his relationship with his wife, and the challenge of his craft. The poems in *Words* make it clear that he will not be satisfied with general assessments and vague phrases. The individual poems in this volume can best be understood and appreciated as elements in a process of self-discovery. Creeley is trying to find out precisely what is important to him about thought, love, and poetry, and what is not important. In a poem from *Words* entitled "I," Creeley thinks about his dead father. He says he feels his father "gave all/ to something like/ the word 'adjoined,' 'extended.' "[1] Which word, Creeley seems to ask in these poems, will best describe the significance of his own life?

This study of Creeley's three major recurrent preoccupations focuses attention on those poems in *Words* considered to be the most important to the development of his themes. In the course of reevaluating life-ordering suppositions concerning the intellect, love, and poetry, Creeley explores the possibilities of the nonintellectual orientation, the solitary existence, and the silent poetic voice. When attention is paid to the poem first as a written object standing free of its context and then as a part of the conceptual whole, we are less likely to misconstrue Creeley's intention. For instance, several poems in *Words* celebrate the irrational; yet it would be wrong to focus on a single such instance and conclude that Creeley ends the argument there. If we recognize the irrational expression as simply one stage in an ongoing consideration of the use and limit of contemplative thought, as one possibility which will in turn be questioned and qualified as a worthwhile mode of perception, we have achieved the proper perspective.

Creeley's central theme in *Words* has to do with the nature of the thinking mind. In his early poems about thinking in *For Love,* Creeley believed intellectual activity to be the activity most worthy of respect and admiration. He felt that a highly disciplined analytical mind, unburdened by preconceived attitudes and assumptions, was potentially capable of understanding the significance of the ordinary moment. The tension in the early poems about thinking derived from the poet's realization that his own intelligence was not nearly as refined as he would have liked it to be. Many of these poems record his false starts and failed efforts to understand. Although Creeley's frustration with the limitations of his own intellectual powers was evident, he never questioned the basic assumption that the ideal mind was in fact a possibility and that the ideal exercise of the intelligence would somehow produce insights into the "truth" of experience. In *Words,* the poems about thinking are filled with frustration and anxiety as well; but in this volume the problems associated with contemplative thought have little to do with the poet's expressed sense of inadequacy and a great deal to do with the limitations peculiar to thought itself.

Creeley challenges his premise that the act of thinking is the most ennobling, satisfying, and purposeful activity. He concludes that the task he imposed on his intellect—the discovery of "truth" or at least "something that would make it all less silly"—is beyond its inherent capability. He discusses the limitations of the rational mind in terms of the hopes he once had for it; and, finally, he experiments with ways to transcend these limitations.

One of the serious dangers the analytical thinker faces is the temptation to study a moment of experience as if it were a problem to be isolated, scrutinized, and solved. If the poet carries this intellectual method of "freezing" the moment to an extreme, he runs the aesthetic risk of cutting his poem off from the flux of experience altogether. M. L. Rosenthal notes Creeley's tendency in his early poems to treat "specific moments of awareness, as if they were totally detachable from the rest of life."[2] Creeley found justification for his method in Paul Valéry's *Monsieur Teste*. Valéry was of course aware of the fact that life changes instant to instant, and thus he advised the poet to be a "Severed Head," a contrivance which would enable him to keep "from merging with change itself" and thereby allow him to explore "the *Capacity* of the moment" at his leisure."[3] Speculation was to be a private activity disassociated from stated intentions, a self-perpetuating process in which new difficulties would be substituted for the satisfaction of attainment, an intellectual exercise fascinating in its own right. In *Words*, the poems about thinking show that Creeley is moving away from Valéry's point of view.

There are many poems in *Words* in which Creeley refers to his habit of treating the act of thinking as a self-sufficient occasion. "Walking" is a reference point in the study of the development of this theme because here the speaker does not question the value of what he is doing. Creeley takes Valéry's advice and images the poet as a "Severed Head":

> Walking
>
> In my head I am
> walking but I am not
> in my head, where
>
> is there to walk,
> not thought of, is
> the road itself more
>
> than seen. I think
> it might be, feel
> as my feet do, and
>
> continue, and
> at least reach, slowly,
> one end of my intention.
>   (p. 36)

Creeley gives the drama of consciousness a physical setting which makes thinking a concrete, palpable actuality. Yet we do not know what he is thinking about or why he is thinking. His "intention" is a private matter. We cannot fault him for not achieving his goal. The poet has, in effect, rid himself of the anxiety usually associated with conventional problem solving. In principle, the speaker will again ask himself "where// is there to walk,/ not thought of" and continue until he reaches another "end" of his "intention." In his preface to *Words*, Creeley defines "intentions" as "the variability of all these feelings, moments of that possibility." As the theme unfolds, Creeley begins to focus attention on the nature of "these feelings" which compelled his thinking at the start.

In "Some Place," Creeley discusses the artificiality of the "detached" milieu from the viewpoint of one who once believed in Valéry's method but who has come, reluctantly indeed, to reject it:

> Some Place
>
> I resolved it, I
> found in my life a
> center and secured it.
>
> It is the house,
> trees beyond, a term
> of view encasing it.
>
> The weather
> reaches only as some
> wind, a little
>
> deadened sighing. And
> if the life weren't?
> when was something to
>
> happen, had I secured
> that—had I, *had*
> I, insistent.
>
> There is nothing I am,
> nothing not. A place
> between, I am. I am
>
> more than thought, less
> than thought. A house
> with winds, but a distance

—something loose in the wind,
feeling weather as that life,
walks toward the lights he left.

(p. 77)

At first a literal setting, "the house" with "trees beyond" quickly
becomes symbolic of the world the poet contrived of his own mind,
an alluring world that exists outside the boundaries of nature. On
the one hand, the poet has created a changeless circumstance in
the romantic tradition and has secured "a term/ of view encasing
it"; on the other hand, he has disassociated himself from the flux of
daily reality, imaged as the weather. The two possibilities are
mutually exclusive. Despite the poet's insistence that he have both,
he must finally choose between living in "a house/ with winds" and
maintaining an intellectual "distance." The poet "walks toward
the lights he left" and the implication is that he will immerse
himself in daily experience.

The emphasis in Creeley's poem is not on the special quality that
distinguishes the "place" from some other place. Rather, the
emphasis is on "a term/ of view encasing it." As Creeley "walks
toward the lights he left," he breaks with Valéry's notion of the
poet as a "Severed Head" coveting his private burden of thought
and moves toward Olson's idea of the poet as an active participant
in the literal world. The poem must vibrate with the energy of life;
Olson advises the poet: "get on with it, keep moving, keep in,
speed, the nerves, the perceptions, theirs, the acts, the split second
acts, the whole business, keep it moving as fast as you can. . . ."4
Words is a transitional volume in Creeley's corpus. At the core of it
is his rejection of Valéry's perspective and his acceptance of
Olson's.

Again and again in *Words*, Creeley refers to his earlier method of
perception. For instance, in "A Birthday": "I had thought/ a
moment of stasis/ possible, some thing fixed—/ days, worlds—." The
curve of feeling in "A Birthday" parallels the shift of attitude in
"Some Place." "A Birthday" ends with the poet's self-critical
realization that "water is wet" and not a subject for endless
contemplation. Although it would have been tempting to "Live/
on the edge" of the world, "looking" (in the poem "Here"), to
contrive a world of one's own mind and look into it "so/ selfishly//
alone," (in the poem "Enough"), and to sustain the "long habit of

much delaying thought/ to savor terms of the impression" (in the poem "A Tally"), it is not possible for him to do so after all. Creeley has lost the confidence he once had that he could scrutinize the "detached" moment and, at the same time, keep pace with the ever-changing reality of experience.

" 'I Keep To Myself Such Measures . . .' " shows the poet forced to confront the fact that his fascination with the "moment of stasis" is leading him towards his own destruction. Creeley's use of the present tense throughout the poem suggests the spontaneity of his realization:

> "I Keep To Myself
> Such Measures . . ."
>
> I keep to myself such
> measures as I care for,
> daily the rocks
> accumulate position.
>
> There is nothing
> but what thinking makes
> it less tangible. The mind,
> fast as it goes, loses
>
> pace, puts in place of it
> like rocks simple markers,
> for a way only to
> hopefully come back to
>
> where it cannot. All
> forgets. My mind sinks.
> I hold in both hands such weight
> it is my only description.
>
> (p. 52)

The poet can store "measures" (stimulating "moment[s] of stasis" in the poem "A Birthday") and label them with "rocks" (tags which will trigger an avalanche of speculation later on), but the mental burden, imaged in physical terms, becomes too heavy. His sense of responsibility to the daily growing pile of "rock"-tagged "measures" nags at him. He cannot ignore these "measures" because the "rocks," like gambling "markers," must be paid. But the mind cannot "come back to// where it cannot." He is committed to his intellectual method; however, he cannot extricate himself from the situation of being in killing debt by resorting to "description" because mere "description" does not take into account the "tangible" nature of the "measure" he once "cared for." Creeley discusses the limitations of the mind in impersonal terms: "There is nothing/ but what thinking makes less tangible. The mind,/ fast as it goes, loses// pace. . . . All/ forgets." He puts his final comment on the mind's inability in personal terms: "My mind sinks." The ideal mind may perhaps exist, but the central point of " 'I Keep To Myself Such Measures . . .' " is that Creeley gives up his hope of attaining it.

The immediacy of felt experience is not accessible to contemplative thought because, as Creeley says in "A Place," "But in the memory I fear// the distortion. I do not feel/ what it was I was feeling." Creeley gives us a more detailed discussion of the dilemma in "Variations." In this poem, the "voice" of "the senses" offers a definition of love which takes love's ever-changing, sensory condition as its essential characteristic. The poet's intellectual attempt to understand what *these senses recreate* is a futile one:

Variations

There is love only
as love is. These
senses recreate
their definition—a hand

holds within itself
all reason. The eyes
have seen such
beauty they close.

But continue. So the voice
again, *these senses recreate*
their singular condition
felt, and felt again.

I hear. I hear
the mind close, the voice
go on beyond it,
the hands open.

> Hard, they hold so
> closely themselves, only,
> empty grasping of
> such sensation.
>
> Hear, there where
> the echoes are
> louder, clearer,
> senses of sound
>
> opening and closing,
> no longer love's
> only, mind's intention,
> eyes' sight, hands holding—
>
> broken to echoes, *these*
> *senses recreate*
> their definition. I hear
> the mind close.
>   (pp. 42–43)

The "senses recreate/ their definition" of "love only/ as love is" at the moment. They have a "voice" which the poet must hear and acknowledge. But the poet's mind, imaged as "a hand" that "holds within itself/ all reason," is determined to isolate the "singular condition" and scrutinize it. The longer the poet contemplates, the further he moves away from the sensory experience which first stimulated his thought. The "hands" are unable to "grasp" the fleeting "sensation" and the "voice," at first heard so distinctly, is at last "broken to echoes." The poet is left to "hear/ the mind close." The felt condition of love, as its definition is recreated by the senses, eludes his understanding.

The limitations of the rational mind is a crucial theme in *Words*. The "detached" milieu is lifeless and the "moment of stasis" is artificial. Then, too, rational thought, by the very nature of its intention, blunts the immediacy of sensory experience and denies the value of the spontaneous impulse. Moreover, Creeley argues, even if he were to accept these limitations, the mind is not capable of remembering clearly what it was it wanted to know about the "detached" moment:

> . . . I
> was always

> thinking. The
> mind itself,
> impulse, of form
>
> last realized,
> nothing
> otherwise but
>
> a stumbling
> looking after. . . .
>   (pp. 69–70)

This passage from "Distance," concerning the distortion and inadequacy bound up with "a stumbling/ looking after," raises yet another danger associated with intellectual activity. The mind may become fascinated by the dynamics of its own process with the result that it may lose interest in its designated object of focus altogether.

Creeley explores this tendency in "The Mountains in the Desert" where the mind, turned hypnotically on itself, comes between the speaker's attentive interest in the mountains and his expected response—the formulation of a thought about them:

> The Mountains
> in the Desert
>
> The mountains blue now
> at the back of my head,
> such geography of self and soul
> brought to such limit of sight,
>
> I cannot relieve it
> nor leave it, my mind locked
> in seeing it
> as the light fades.
>
> Tonight let me go
> at last out of whatever
> mind I thought to have,
> and all the habits of it.
>   (p. 23)

At the start, the contemplative mind focuses on the actually unseen mountains. Scrutiny begins at dusk, "the mountains blue now," and continues "as the light fades." Theoretically, this mental process can go on forever because the activity has nothing to do with seeing the mountains. The poet's intellect has transcended the "limit of sight" and, more to the point, it has rid itself of the anxiety usually associated with formulating an insight based on accurate description. Thought is attractively self-sufficient.

In the second stanza, the poet turns his attention to the nature of the intellectual activity itself. He finds that he has lost control of it and a confrontation is building between the endless stare bound up with the "geography of self and soul" and the recognizably human look dependent on literal time and space. The poet is being caught up in a consideration of the dynamics of his own thinking. He has forgotten or no longer cares about the "mountains in the desert." His concern is with the kind of intellectual exercise that is self-engaged and self-perpetuating. It has become a trap, a "habit" which blocks his purpose:

> Tonight let me go
> at last out of whatever
> mind I thought to have,
> and all the habits of it.

Creeley is not arguing for a completely nonintellectual perspective. The poems in *Words* show him reevaluating "habits" of thought. He recognizes the limitations inherent in thinking "a moment of stasis/ possible" (from "A Birthday"), in assuming the proper exercise of the intelligence would lead him to the discovery of "truth," and in believing the activity of the mind to be a fascinating process which ought therefore to be cultivated and appreciated apart from any practical considerations. To deal with these limitations, Creeley introduces new methods of perception into his poetic universe. He records the spontaneous impulse in very short poems, takes the "shift and drift" of illogical associations into account in very long poems divided into parts, and allows the anger, barely beneath the surface in the early poems, to spend itself in explicitly violent imagery. The most successful poetic result of Creeley's reorientation is *Pieces,* a long sequence in which a wide variety of modes of perception are used. In *Words*, we have the beginning of Creeley's attempt to tap his intuitions, emotions, and impulses for his poetry.

The poetry of spontaneous impulse or, as Creeley puts it, the

poetry of "*scribbling,* of writing for the immediacy of the pleasure
without having to pay attention to some final code of significance,"[5] becomes an added condition of expressed awareness that
has value in Creeley's new point of view. We get brief poems like:

> A Piece
> One and
> one, two,
> three.
>
>   (p. 115)

As this form appears in *Words,* without benefit of context or
comment, it seems simply a curiosity. Yet Creeley speaks with high
seriousness about the importance of this poem: "When *Words* was
published, I was interested to see that one of the poems most
irritating to reviewers was 'A Piece'—and yet I knew that for me it
was central to all possibilities of statement."[6]

"A Piece" is a reference point in the study of Creeley's poetry
because of the possibilities for poetic expression implicit in its
making. Creeley discusses its composition in terms of his previous
attitude—"I had trusted so much to *thinking*"[7]—and his present
attitude, which takes into account the limitations bound up with
intellectual activity. We must go to Creeley's discussion of the
writing of "A Piece" rather than to the poem itself if we are to
understand why this is a key poem.

In a conversation with Allen Ginsberg, taped at the University of
British Columbia Poetry Conference in 1963, Creeley describes the
physical condition in which the early poems were written as a
rigidly organized condition he hoped would assure him of his own
professionalism and assure others of his seriousness.[8] In a postscript
to this conversation, written five years later, Creeley recalls his talk
with Ginsberg as an occasion that changed his future as a writer.
He says that during this conversation he realized that the specific
work situation he had created and held on to limited the kinds of
feelings coming into it and hence into the poems. He goes on to
say:

> Not long after I began to try deliberately to break out of the
> habits described. I wrote in different states of so-called
> consciousness. e.g. when high, and at those times would write
> in pen or pencil, contrary to habit, and I would also try to

avoid any immediate decision as to whether or not the effects of such writings were "good." Some of the poems so written are to be found in *Words,* among them "A Piece," "The Box," "They (2)," and "The Farm."[9]

In 1963 Creeley began to use notebooks in which he set down thoughts and feelings as they occurred to him on the spot. The poetic result is a spontaneous recording of insights and impressions, which differs, of course, from an intellectual assessment of a past experience. The poems collected in *Words* were written between the beginning of 1961 and the end of 1966. They are arranged in more or less chronological order, and so it is not surprising that as we move toward the end of the volume we find more poems which evidence Creeley's more flexible method of composition. Speaking about this new-found sense of freedom, Creeley says: "It's lovely to do something with your bare hands and mind, in the instant it *is* possible, and finally I know it."[10]

"A Piece," then, represents Creeley's discovery that the deliberately nonintellectual vantage point has its value. The "mind" will continue to be the shaping power behind the poem, but hereafter it will incorporate the spontaneous impulse and the irrational insight into the structure of the poem. Whereas short poems like "A Piece" show that Creeley is beginning to make use of a wider variety of modes of articulation than before, long poems show that he is working out new methods of organization to serve his expanded poetic sensibility.

In an interview with Linda Wagner, Creeley speaks about his early "habits of organization," in which "continuity . . . was taken pretty directly from the rhetorical terms of thesis, antithesis, etc." He says he learned "how to *continue*" by writing his only novel, *The Island,* in 1962. The longer poems in *Words* show that he "found how things could drift and shift, and how the line might encompass that possibility":

> "Anger" or "Distance" or "The Dream" or "The Woman"— all of these were written after the novel, and all demonstrate that there's a possibility of going on in the poem that hadn't been there previously. There are only a few poems of this order prior to the novel—one is "The Door," but even so its sequence is determined by an almost rhetorical term of argument.[11]

Free from a structural pattern in which the "sequence is determined by an almost rhetorical term of argument," Creeley allows
his thoughts and feelings to "shift and drift" around a unifying
preoccupation in the poem. The result is a poem no longer tied to
the "thesis-antithesis" process of thought but closer to the complexity of an ordinary moment of experience.

In each of the four poems Creeley points to as illustrative
products of his new organizational method, we get a seemingly
simultaneous comprehension of the speaker's intellectual and
sensory perceptions. There was a great deal of simmering emotion,
particularly anger, just beneath the surface of Creeley's early,
ironic poems. In "Anger," one of the long poems in *Words*, Creeley
deals explicitly with his feelings and his thoughts about his feeling
as parts of an inextricably bound whole. This poem shows what
Creeley has gained from his experiments with the brief record of
spontaneous impulse and with the associational pattern of organization.

"Anger" is a dramatic lyric about a husband's night-long
argument with his wife. In the first lines of this six-part poem, the
time of the action is set ("The time is"), the scene is described
("The air seems a cover,/ the room is quiet"), and the two
unnamed characters are introduced ("She moves, she/ had moved.
He/ heard her"). We are told that the children are asleep and the
dog is fed. Such assurance in Creeley's poetry is typically a prelude
to some kind of divergent behavior. In the poem at hand, the
husband's anger disrupts the scene. Part 1 of "Anger" follows:

1
The time is.
The air seems a cover,
the room is quiet.

She moves, she
had moved. He
heard her.

The children
sleep, the dog fed,
the house around them

is open, descriptive,
a truck through the walls,
lights bright there,

glaring, the sudden
roar of its motor, all
familiar impact

as it passed
so close. He
hated it.

But what does she answer.
She moves
away from it.

In all they save,
in the way of his saving
the clutter, the accumulation

of the expected disorder—
as if each dirtiness,
each blot, blurred

happily, gave
purpose, happily—
she is not enough there.

He is angry. His
face grows—as if
a moon rose

of black light,
convulsively darkening,
as if life were black.

It is black.
It is an open
hole of horror, of

nothing as if not
enough there is
nothing. A pit—

which he recognizes,
familiar, sees
the use in, a hole

for anger and
fills it
with himself,

yet watches on
the edge of it,
as if she were

not to be pulled in,
a hand could
stop him. Then

as the shouting
grows and grows
louder and louder

with spaces
of the same open
silence, the darkness,

in and out, him-
self between them,
stands empty and

holding out his
hands to both,
now screaming

it cannot be
the same, she
waits in the one

while the other
moans in the hold
in the floor, in the wall.
                    (pp. 62–64)

Part 1 begins with a simple, recognizably human situation. The husband wants his wife to share his frustrations but "she moves/

away from it. . . . she is not enough there." Then Creeley
gradually involves us in a more imaginative and ambiguous
circumstance. The husband's "face grows—as if/ a moon rose// of
black light." The metaphor is provocative. "Rose" might be a verb
or a noun or a displaced adjective. Although each of the three
interpretations makes literal sense, "rose," given the context, must
be a verb. Yet Creeley has made his point by slowing down the
pace of the poem: each reading is just credible enough to make the
careful reader pause if only for a moment. He uses the single word
with several possible grammatical functions to comment on the
complexity of the issue. And, too, he uses the pause to brake the
action while he directs us away from the familiarly lifelike and
easily knowable and prepares us for something else.

At the start, the husband is presented as a single human being.
He then splits in two and becomes a self divided against itself. He is
both the plaintiff and the judge in his quarrel with his wife. Creeley
will use this technique to dramatize opposed elements of his own
personality, a technique rooted in his heretofore fundamental but
now qualified assumption that the mind in conversation with itself
is the most special occasion. When we overheard the speaker
talking to himself in the early poems, we could not predict his
mood. From this point on in Creeley's poems, when we catch a
speaker talking to himself we know he feels awkward at best,
hopelessly despondent at worst.

The husband's intellectual and sensory perceptions, whether
they are based on the actual or on the fantastic, are both in
evidence in Part 1 of "Anger." Creeley juxtaposes thought and
feeling in each of the five remaining sections of the poem. For
instance in Part 2, the husband casts about for an appropriate
equivalent for "rage" and then follows this intellectual attempt
with a comment on the inadequacy of these thoughts: "I think I
think/ but find myself in it." Finally he concludes the passage with
an outburst: "I rage./ I rage, I rage." Similarly in Part 4, the
speaker's comments about what he sees and hears and feels are
interspersed with his thoughts about the significance of his sensory
experience. The same pattern is repeated throughout the poem.
The central point about this balanced interplay is that Creeley
brings together thought and feeling for the first time in his poetry in
an explicit way.

Creeley finds that the ordinary moment of experience is a

mysteriously complex occasion and that his response to it is filled with intellectual contractions and often disturbing impulses, as "Anger" makes plain. There are poems in *Words* that go well beyond "Anger" in taking account of the speaker's violent urges. "Hello" is a fine example, and as such it stands at the furthest remove from "Walking," a poem which assumed intellectual activity to be the desired, all-absorbing pursuit. In black-humored "Hello," the speaker catches the woman's eye and makes his presence felt:

> Hello
>
> With a quick
> jump he caught
> the edge of
>
> her eye and
> it tore, down,
> ripping. She
>
> shuddered,
> with the unexpected
> assault, but
>
> to his vantage
> he held by
> what flesh was left.
>
> (p. 40)

"Hello" has the distinction of being the most vicious poem in the whole of Creeley's work. Creeley's loss of an eye is well known and the personal tragedy gives the bizarre greeting a literal base of interest for informed readers. The essential impact of the poem, however, comes from the distressing sense of the words supported by the falling sounds of "her eye and/ it tore, down,/ ripping" in a concentrated field of dentates and plosives. If Creeley barely escaped the consequences of putting too much faith in contemplative thought, he falls into the trap of celebrating the violent assault apart from and without an attempt to understand it in "Hello."

"Hello" is one extreme in Creeley's consideration of his central theme, the nature of the active mind. The poems in *Words* that shape the development of this motif—"Walking," "Some Place," " 'I Keep to Myself Such Measures . . . ,' " "Variations," "The Mountains in the Desert," "Anger," and "Hello"—show the poet asking specific questions about contemplative thought: what is its potential? its limitation? its proper aim? He finds that he was wrong to contrive a world of his own mind, to think "a moment of stasis/ possible" (from "A Birthday"), to ignore the sensory perception and to deny the value of the spontaneous impulse. He finds that he is caught up in the flux of daily reality and that he must make us believe that he is faithfully recording insights and feelings as they occur to him. Creeley is working toward a conceptual framework and a poetic structure in which a wide variety of modes of perception have value and place. Contemplative thought still retains its position in Creeley's poetic universe as the most highly valued mode of perception but the poems in *Words* speak to his realization that there is "much else" that is inaccessible to thought.

His various attempts to find a coherent pattern to his life and to secure a meaningful self-definition involve a reassessment of previous attitudes. His effort to understand what love can accomplish and what it cannot emerges from the poems in *Words* to become a major theme. Creeley once believed naïvely in love. The fundamental assumption in his early poems about love, collected in *For Love,* was that a love relationship was a possibility, an ideal condition. If he could attain it, the basic implication continued, he would be able to make sense of his experience. Although his early poems about love and marriage are filled with posturing—addresses to an unapproachable, idealized woman at one end of the spectrum and contemptuous rejections of a cruelly insensitive woman at the other—they are after all poignant pleas for love. Whereas the poems in *Words* show Creeley still looking for "measures—/ ways of being in one's life" (from "For Joel"), they show him wondering if love is enough, if love is equal to the task he imposed on it. He finds that he can learn about the dynamics of a love relationship and that he can express his thoughts and feelings about a recognizably human woman more honestly and directly than before, but that he cannot believe love to be a mystical power capable of infusing ordinary experience with the kind of satisfying meaning he once hoped for.

Creeley's fundamental assumption about love changes as does his basic attitude toward marriage. In *Words,* he is still writing poems for love but he is talking about achieving a manageable, working relationship. Comments about married love are scattered throughout this volume, both in poems that are primarily about the subject and in poems that deal chiefly with Creeley's other major preoccupations—the act of thinking and the act of poem-making. We can study Creeley's treatment of the love motif in "Enough," a long poem in which he brings together all of the important aspects of the theme as it is developed in *Words*.

Formally, the poem is a narrative lyric: the protagonist wants a happily peaceful relationship with his wife, a woman who, by her silence, seems indifferent to his hope. The emphasis in the poem is on the husband's tense voice. In each of the poem's six sections, he discusses his inability to communicate effectively with his wife and he explores various alternatives for dealing with the problem. The moment of crisis comes in Section 5 when the husband faces "the pain of the impossible understanding" that his wife is either actually unfaithful to him or at least would like to be; the resolution of the conflict comes in Section 6 when the protagonist resigns himself to staying in the relationship as it is.

"Enough" opens with a stated defense of poetry. The speaker says that the poem is the appropriate vehicle for his thoughts and feelings because it makes a "common// ground." We are left to wonder if he is speaking as the poet and referring to the "common// ground" between the writer and reader or if he is speaking as the husband and referring to his need to communicate with his wife in a mode "prized enough" by the outside world. Both possibilities are present:

1

It is possible, in words, to speak
of what has happened—a sense

of there and here, now
and then. It is some other

way of being, prized enough,
that it makes a common

ground. Once
you were

alone and I
met you. It was late

at night.
I never

left after that,
not to my own mind,

but stayed
and stayed. Years

went by. What
were they. Days—

some happy
but some bitter

and sad. If I walked
across the room, then,

and saw you un-
expected, saw the particular

whiteness of
your body, a little

older, more
tired—in words

I possessed it, in
my mind I thought, and

you never knew
it, there I danced

for you, stumbling, in
the corner of my eye.

                    (pp. 122–23)

The opening conversational tone quickly becomes tense as the
speaker tells about their first meeting, his commitment to the
woman, and his inability to communicate with her. The sense of
nervousness is conveyed by the heavily stressed, choppy lines which
break unnaturally at the adjective or at the preposition. Most of the
lines contain interior punctuation and they become, in effect, short

gasps. Creeley plays these broken lines off against a tightly
interwoven, even sound pattern made up of consonantal and
vocalic echoes, repeated monosyllables, and parallel constructions.
The poetic result of this interplay is to underscore the speaker's
difficulty in saying what would normally be considered a matter-of-
fact statement:

>   . . . Once
> you were
>
> alone and I
> met you. It was late
>
> at night.

The husband is gradually building up to a confession: he cannot
talk to her because of his own self-protective habit of transposing
thoughts and feelings into words left unsaid. There is the suggestion
that he is made speechless by the surprise of seeing her "unexpected" or sidetracked into a silent consideration by the sight of
her "body, a little// older, more/ tired." By the close of the first
section of "Enough," however, the speaker comes to the reason
why "some other/ way of being" is needed to make "a common//
ground." He cannot respond to the woman because he has
contrived a world of his mind.

In this place of personalized consciousness he "danced . . .
stumbling," an action representative of the usual mix of affection
and frustration characteristic of a usual relationship. But the
woman "never knew/ it." She did know his sarcasm or his
adoration. Although we can find instances to the contrary, the
women in Creeley's early poems were either victimized or
worshipped. In the midsections of "Enough" the speaker struggles
with his old habits of mind—a struggle that is, of course, relevant to
the outcome of the poem at hand, and, in a larger sense, a struggle
that marks a turning point in Creeley's treatment of the love motif.

As Creeley puts it in Part 3 of "Enough," it was his habit to
envision a sunlit "golden city," a world in which her "eyes once/ in
words were// lakes." At the other extreme, it was his habit to
imagine a dark, obscene place filled with "Hoo, hoo—/ laughter"
(Part 4). Either way he had made "a picture// for the world/ to
be" (Part 5), and either way he was alone and unsatisfied. The

"golden city" was after all a vague place in which the actual woman was not present: "I// try to feel/ where you are" (Part 3). Similarly, in the made place in which he could "see// the obscene bodies/ twisting, twisting" and "explore their/ delight, un-/noticed," he could not participate fully: "my body// shrinks/ back" (Part 4). The husband wants to communicate with his wife, but before he can do so he must recognize the artificiality of his old habits. In the words of the poem, he must give up the "golden city" and the obscene place and live instead in the actual world, the world of the "stumbling" dance. Compelled by loneliness to change his "way of being," the speaker first defines his attitude toward his wife in terms of his old habits and then deals with his fears in human terms:

7

Your body is a garbage can.
Your body is white, why

let others touch it, why
not. Why

my body so
tentative, do I

like the pain
of such impossible understanding.

Your body
is a white

softness, it has
its own

place time
after time.

(p. 127)

"Enough" is an important poem in a study of Creeley's poetry for two reasons. From this point on, he presents credible human women and he discusses his thoughts and feelings about them in explicitly human terms. If Creeley makes an exception to this general pattern, he will tell us clearly in the poem itself that he is fantasizing about women within the context of a dream or of a drug-induced state. Closely associated with this decision to portray lifelike women is his reassessment of his heretofore fundamental assumption that love is a mystical force capable of infusing ordinary experience with transcendent meaning. In the final section of "Enough," the husband rededicates himself to his marriage. Love, as he can ever hope to understand it, is a complex bond between two people and it is only that:

8

I vow to my life to respect it.
I will not wreck it.

I vow to yours to be ⌐
enough, enough, enough.

(p. 127)

Over and again in *Words* Creeley says that he tested his belief in the power of love against his actual experience and found that his hope was an illusion. He cannot find profound inspiration in love any more than he can find complete understanding by virtue of analytical thinking. All he can do is live each moment as it comes and bear witness to what he feels and what he thinks about his experience in the poem. Creeley puts it this way in his preface to *Words:* "So it is that what I feel, in the world, is the one thing I know myself to be, for that instant. I will never know myself otherwise." We get poems, then, in which Creeley records an "instant" of his experience, wonders about its significance, and resigns himself to not knowing.

Creeley's attitude toward his poem is the third major issue in *Words.* He focuses attention on the process of writing a poem from the point of view of a careful poet who is actively engaged in the process of poem making. He invites the reader to collaborate with him, to help him think through his technical problems. He involves us in the activity of composition by opening the poem to include the dynamics of its making. We are frustrated when he is frustrated and satisfied when he is satisfied. We come to realize that he is compelled to write; there is "no meaning,/ no point" in any systematic sense. In his preface to *Words,* the seasoned craftsman lays his assessment of the value his poetry has for him on the aesthetic line: "I am trying to say that what I think to say is of no help to me—and yet insist on my seriousness, which is a sense of my nature I would like to admire." For Creeley, the poem is a necessity. His plainly honest discernment of that unpretentious fact and its implications generates and governs this *ars poetica* motif.

There are many poems in *Words* which, to use Duncan's phrase, are poems of linguistic impulse. Of these poems which disclose the poet's frustrating experience with verbs, nouns, subjects, and tenses—their multifacted nature as well as their arrangement—the one which lays bare the confusions involved most plainly is:

> For W. C. W.
>
> The rhyme is after
> all the repeated
> insistence.
>
> There, you say, and
> there, and there,
> and *and* becomes
>
> just so. And
> what one wants is
> what one wants,
>
> yet complexly
> as you
> say.
>
> Let's
> let it go.
> I want—
>
> Then there is—
> and,
> I want.
>
> (p. 27)

The poem truly pays homage to William Carlos Williams. Creeley praises Williams's ability to record the continuity of experience faithfully and, at the same time, to delineate the uniqueness of each instant precisely. The lesson Creeley is reluctantly learning from

Williams has to do with finding the exact word and setting it in the poem "just so." "For W. C. W." argues that there are three methods for conveying recurrence: rhymed words suggest correspondence, as do parallel constructions and repetitions. Yet nothing can happen quite as it did before. It is the poet's difficult task to make fine distinctions. "What one wants is" is not the same as "what one wants"; similarly, there is a substantial difference between "I want—" and "I want." The tedious decisions that go into shaping raw material into a finished product are discussed within a humorous context. We can imagine Williams insisting on the complexity of the problem and Creeley resisting instruction: "Let's/ let it go."

In "Waiting," treacherous words, unyielding and perhaps inadequate to the occasion compelling artistic release, are formidable obstacles to the resolute poet, barely able yet surely driven to apprehend the occasion and find its verbal equivalent. Creeley strips his poetic posture down to its motivational mandate. There are no humorous touches in this poem to relieve the tension created by the poet's desperate mood.

Waiting

He pushes behind the words
which, awkward, catch
and turn him to a disturbed
and fumbling man.

What if it all stops.
Then silence
is as silence was
again.

What if the last time
he was moved to touch,
work out in his own mind,
such limits was the last—

and then a quiet, a dull
space of hanging actions, all
depending on some time
has come and gone.

God help him then
if such things can.
That risk
is all there is.

(p. 24)

The confused push and shove of difficult entrance is captured by
the first stanza's ambiguous syntax. We learn later that silence
literally forces the poet to speech, that for him thinking, feeling,
and writing are interrelated, actually interdependent elements of a
single impulse. But who "pushes behind the words" in the first
place? Is it the "disturbed// and fumbling" poet or someone else
who entrusts the "awkward" words to his care? Are the words
unwieldy or is he clumsy? The frustrations are real and the blame
must be shared. Yet without words, the poet goes on, we not only
have "silence" but "a dull/ space of hanging actions," which exist
mechanically in time. The customary invocation to the Muse is
cynically reduced to a rhetorical gesture: "God help him then/ if
such things can." Without blessed inspiration and its sustaining
assurance, the poet will "risk" pushing and catching words because
it is for whatever reason the condition of his life.

"The Language," like "Waiting," derives its meaning from its
actual coming into being. Here again creative activity is compelled
by silence, but this time the poetic focus plays on a specific, sensual
instance of symbiotic violation, the prelude to expression:

The Language

Locate *I*
love you some-
where in

teeth and
eyes, bite
it but

take care not
to hurt, you
want so

much so
little. Words
say everything,

I
love you
again,

then what
is emptiness
for. To

fill, fill.
I heard words
and words full

of holes
aching. Speech
is a mouth.
                    (p. 37)

The poet and the words, mutually absorbed in a physical, repetitive process, testify to their interdependence. "The Language" ends on the verge of statement: the "words full// of holes/ aching," the "mouth" ready to fill silence with "*I/ love you.*" The emphasis in the poem is on the intensity and nature of the pleasure-pain relationship. The implication is that prestatement preparation, like sexual foreplay, to which it is compared, is an activity deserving at least some attention. The poem records the dynamics of its own making and nothing more.

Language is an intangible concept. In "For W. C. W.," "Waiting," and more clearly in "The Language," Creeley is trying to isolate the substantial aspect of words. If he can grip the substance of words, he can deal with them in the same way that he can deal with any other concrete actuality. In *Homage to Creeley* (1960–61), Jack Spicer has a great deal of fun with Creeley's hope that words, in the hands of a poet, are or can possibly be tangible commodities. Consider the first stanza of Spicer's poem entitled "Magic":

> Strange, I had words for dinner
> Stranger, I had words for dinner
> Stranger, strange, do you believe me?[12]

It is interesting to read Creeley's poem "The Language" (1963) as a response to "Magic." Whereas Spicer seems amused by Creeley's intent, the poems about poetry in *Words* show that Creeley is absolutely serious. He would eat words and he would drink words. He would hold holy intercourse with them. They are the condition of his life.

"The Language" is chiefly about the poetic process. Yet Creeley's use of self-directed questions and admonitions as well as his use of sexual imagery in the poem recall his other major themes at the same time. We can learn more about Creeley's interest in dealing with several issues as parts of an interrelated whole from his introduction to *Whitman Selected by Robert Creeley*. He says that contemporary American poets "can no longer assume either their world or themselves in it as discrete occasion."[13] although he once did so:

> I had grown up, so to speak, habituated to the use of poetry as compact, epiphanal instance of emotion or insight. I valued its intensive compression, its ability to "get through" a maze of conflict and confusion to some centre of clear "point." But what did one do if the emotion or terms of thought could not be so focused upon or isolated in such singularity? Assuming a context of necessity multiphasic, a circumstance the components of which were multiple, or, literally, a day in which various things *did* occur, not simply one thing—what did one do with that?[14]

Creeley goes on to say that he learned from Whitman not to think of a poem as a "discreet line through alternatives to some adamant point of conclusion"[15] but rather to think of a poem as an "agglomerative" composition. Creeley defines "agglomerative" in terms of what he believes to be Whitman's basic pattern of organization. "Agglomerative" is "that sense of the spherical, which does not locate itself upon a point nor have the strict condition of the linear but rather is at all 'points' the possibility of all that it is."[16]

Creeley uses the "agglomerative" pattern in *Words*. Although most of the poems in this volume are addressed to the "discrete occasion" of thinking, love, or the creative process, several poems deal with these three themes simultaneously. "The Language," "Joy," and "Some Echoes" are a few such "braided" poems. "Words," the title poem, deserves special attention because it is Creeley's most fully developed "multiphasic" statement and thus it is a fine place to sum up what has happened thematically in *Words*.

Creeley's three major themes are intertwined and resolved in the title poem of the volume. Although "Words" is a "braided" poem, its central focus has to do with Creeley's deep commitment to his craft. The poem is a sophisticated apostrophe in which the poet addresses his medium with loving respect, fully conscious of the frustration of waiting for words.

Words

You are always
with me,
there is never
a separate

place. But if
in the twisted
place I
cannot speak,

not indulgence
or fear only,
but a tongue
rotten with what

it tastes— There is
a memory
of water, of
food, when hungry.

Some day
will not be
this one, then
to say

words like a
clear, fine
ash sifts,
like dust,

from nowhere.
(p. 92)

Creeley is too experienced with words to accept the aesthetics of silence naïvely. A poetic posture which asserts its authority by refusing to say what it surely, obviously knows may well be a sincere and authentic one. But for him it is not. When his "tongue" is "rotten with what// it tastes," there perhaps ought to be words as something at least to say; yet he cannot find them. If he "cannot speak" it may be that he is indulging his compulsion to search out the precise innuendo and the most effective construction. If he "cannot speak" it may be because he is afraid. Words are ultimately mysterious elements which may mock his intention to manipulate them. The poet wants to possess words, but he discovers that words will not be possessed; like "ash," they cannot be eaten. He admits to his presumption and to his awkwardness; yet he remains essentially confident. "Some day," he says, words, the drift of them, will naturally, miraculously be given to him.

Creeley's attitude toward his poem is a major issue in the volume. Every important aspect of the theme appears in "Words." The curve of feeling in this poem parallels the development of the love motif as well. Creeley wanted his marriage to be a mystical circumstance in which husband and wife became one, but later comes to realize that his wife has her own identity and that he has his own identity. Love between two people is a complex bond; it is not a condition of ownership. "Words" is a love lyric. It begins with a statement about oneness: "You are always/ with me,/ there is never/ a separate// place" and it ends with the poet's realization that words do not belong to him: "words like a/ clear, fine/ ash sifts,/ like dust,// from nowhere."

Of Creeley's three major themes in *Words*, the central one involves his assessment of the uses and the limitations of thought. He once hoped that he would gain an insight into the "truth" of his experience by the proper exercise of his intelligence. To contemplate the significance of a past event was of value, surely, but only up to a point. When thinking became an intricate, self-challenging game, it lost its value as a mode of perception. "Words" is a "braided" poem in which Creeley recapitulates the story of his struggle to set intellectual activity into the proper perspective. The peom begins with a thesis statement which is followed by an antithetical statement.

You are always
with me,
there is never
a separate

place. But if
in the twisted
place I
cannot speak. . . .

The poet starts to analyze the contradiction in terms of his "indulgence," "fear," and bitter experience. He breaks off his speculation abruptly. His subject is "words" and his thoughts are leading him away from it. He can take a general sense of hope and comfort from the memory of past satisfactions. But he must not distort or complicate his present concern by lingering in the recollection. Instead, he looks forward to the future: "Some day/ will not be/ this one." All in all, he must simply wait. "Words" will come from "nowhere," the name William Morris gave to his Utopia. Morris excluded brilliant truth-tellers from *Nowhere*, a perfect place where intricate speculating is not allowed. The final sense of the volume as well as of the title poem is that Creeley, too, has decided to leave out thought-fighting. He is beginning to put faith in his intuition.

3

PIECES

"... pitiful
the world's
lonely who
would love all"
            —Louis Zukofsky, *A-19*

Like the poems in *For Love* and *Words,* the long sequence *Pieces*
is about the nature of the thinking mind, the poetic process, and
the love relationship. Here Creeley reworks his basic themes; his
purpose is to formulate a self-definition that will enable him to feel
at home with himself and at home in the world. We can better
understand Creeley's ideas as he develops them in *Pieces* by first
reviewing his treatment of these themes in the past.

In his earliest poems about thinking, Creeley was taken with the
possibility that a clear and refined intellect might learn the secrets
of the mysterious forces that control the apparently meaningless
and often distressing phenomenal world. He concluded that his
hope to make sense of everyday confusions and dilemmas in this
way was a cruel illusion. Then, in *Words,* he examined the
dynamics of his own thinking process with a view toward
discerning what in his experience was accessible to rational
thought and what was not. He found that intuition was a mode of
perception he could trust and a necessary complement to his
logical habits of mind. In *Pieces,* Creeley tries to bring the analytical
and the intuitive into a proper balance, the result of this fusion to
be a more complete and thus more valid method of ordering
experience than his previous one.

Closely related to Creeley's critical interest in his imagination is

85

his attempt to understand the various aspects of the poet's role. He speculates on the mysterious source of the poet's authority; he considers the frustrating relationship between the well-intentioned poet committed to the careful practice of his craft and the uncomprehending reader too lazy to follow the poem's meaning; finally, he assesses his poetic achievement, in terms of its value as a doctrinal statement and its worth as an amusing distraction. Although he has raised questions about these matters before in the poems about poetry in *For Love* and *Words,* he seems more determined to explore the issues fully and to settle the answers firmly in *Pieces.*

The third major theme in *Pieces* has to do with the philosophical significance of the love relationship. Philosophical significance was not a concern in the early poems in which Creeley focused on the tensions associated with his first marriage, divorce, and remarriage. It was a concern in *Words* where he contemplated his relationship with his second wife: he might derive comfort and pleasure from his marriage in the ordinary sense, he concluded, but he could not find satisfaction in metaphysical terms. In *Pieces,* Creeley struggles to reconcile his empirical understanding that he is essentially alone in this world with his recognizably human need to feel a sense of belonging. Incapable or unwilling to put his faith in love, he searches for some other reassurance that the "singleness" he "make[s] an evidence/ has purpose."[1] Failing this, he tries to redefine his attitude toward love.

Poetry, love, and thinking do not exist simply as independent motifs in *Pieces;* rather, they are actually interdependent, joined in a kind of "agglomerative" union (discussed in Chapter 2), so that fluctuations in one result in variations in the other. Creeley develops these intertwined themes within the context of the romance convention, and the following analysis makes use of the terms Northrop Frye uses to describe the romance in *The Anatomy of Criticism.* The hero of *Pieces* undertakes a perilous journey which breaks into three distinct parts, each introudced by his descent into an area of his experience. The nature of his descent comments on his mood and, at the same time, establishes the ambience of the places he visits. For instance, the first descent finds him awkwardly and cautiously approaching the middle of his own person. He goes on to describe what is closest to him, his immediate family situation and his mysterious birth as a storyteller.

The second descent takes him into the more dangerous milieu of personal relationships, both social and intellectual. His third descent is an explicitly treacherous one. It brings him to the hell-town of Chicago and from there to contemporary American society as a whole.

With the perilous journey over, the hero confronts his enemy, a sea monster who "devoured us all." In the course of three separate attempts to subdue the monster the hero gradually realizes that he himself is the source of his predicament. The sea creature disappears, leaving the hero to review his thoughts about the nature of the imagination, the poet's burden, and the value of love. His victory takes place in his own mind; his reward illustrates what he has learned. First through prayer and humility and then (in the volume's final poem) "after drinking and/ talking," he is able to approach "the goddess or woman// become her," the symbol in *Pieces* of a permanent mysterious force as well as the image of a desirable human woman. Their union, both metaphysical and earthy, completes the story. In the tradition of romance, Creeley's speaker then yields his place to the reader and ask that another tale be told.

The romance convention is firm enough to establish structural unity yet flexible enough to allow for a wide range of possibilities through which Creeley can develop his themes. The hero of *Pieces*, who serves to mediate the complexities of our time by questioning the cause of his restlessness and ours, has many different kinds of experiences and tells about them in a variety of ways. He is, nonetheless, a single recognizable character because his disparate actions are contained within the single all-embracing metaphor of the quest-journey. Supporting details, such as repeated references to his two-dimensional sight and his recurrent preoccupations, help identify him as well. Without the stabilizing context of the quest-journey, however, these details might be lost in the welter of random associations, abrupt transitions, and startling contrasts of the episodic form. In the episodic form, as Creeley works with it, narrative, chronological, and logical unity are ignored, and events are not put into proper perspective, with irrelevancies discarded and cause-and-effect relations established. Yet the romance has its own definite sequence, which Creeley exploits, thus gaining a cohesive pattern for material that would be otherwise disorganized.

Perhaps an even more important aspect of the romance is that it is traditionally meant to create *wonder*. *Pieces* creates the illusion that we are participating in an amazing process, that we are with the puzzled hero considering the evidence, venturing hypotheses, and at last offering a conceptual generalization that takes account of the disjunct pieces. This atmosphere of fantasy that pervades the sequence offsets the seriousness of the hero's attempt to infuse the " 'breathtaking banalities' " (p. 41) of his life with meaning. His solution to the *"mystery . . . involved"* (p. 33) is presented finally as an entertaining possibility rather than a didactic answer, a direct result of Creeley's decision to emphasize the wondrous nature of the story.

The opening poem of the sequence introduces the several themes with which Creeley will be concerned, and the focus is on his casually confident approach. In "As real as thinking," the enthusiastic poet outlines his intention to create a wondrous "sentence," a "present" made up of the play of thought that is to be both useful and pleasurable (in the tradition of Horace's dictum).

> As real as thinking
>
> As real as thinking
> wonders created
> by the possibility—
>
> forms. A period
> at the end of a sentence
> which
>
> began *it was*
> into a present,
> a presence
>
> saying
> something
> as it goes.
>
> .
>
> No forms less
> than activity.
>
> All words—
> days—or
> eyes—

or happening
is an event only
for the observer?

No one
there. Everyone
here.

             •

Small facts
of eyes, hair
blonde, face

looking like a
flat painted
board. How

opaque as if
a reflection
merely, skin

vague glove of
randomly seen
colors.
     . . . . . (pp. 3–4)

The idea that the poet is a dabbling amateur content to offer us a
sentence that merely says "something/ as it goes" is countered by
his promise to create "wonders," a promise conveyed by the
specific literary allusions in the passage as well as by the implied
ones. The most prominently placed reference is to Louis Zukofsky's
It Was which, together with the fact that the sequence is dedicated
to him, suggests Creeley's felt affinity with the avowed purpose of
Zukofsky's work. Zukofsky writes in *It Was:*

> This story was a story of our time. And a writer's attempts not
> to fathom his time amount but to sounding his mind in it. I did
> not want to break up my form by pointing to well-known
> place names and dates in the forty years that I had lived—
> events familiar to most of us, to some more than myself. I
> wanted our time to be the story, but like the thought of a
> place passed by once and recalled altogether: seen again as
> through a stereoscope blending views a little way apart into a

solid—defying touch. I was saying something that had had a
sequence, like the knowledge of taking a breath, and hiding it,
because one breathes without pointing to it before and after.
Having tortured myself most of the night to get down just that
in one sentence of my story, I hoped that the freedom of the
green, the sun and the air of the park would make the task
easier.[2]

Creeley's "sentence," the image of his sequence, begins *"it was";*
the effect of this allusion is to bring his poem—a wonder "created/
by the possibility" of thinking—and Zukofsky's story, in which "a
writer's attempts not to fathom his time amount but to sounding his
mind in it," into a single frame of reference. Whereas Zukofsky
candidly admits to "having tortured myself most of the night to get
down just that in one sentence of my story," Creeley insists on the
spontaneity of his effort by relegating the issue of high seriousness
to literary allusions.

In the first sections of "As real as thinking," Creeley maintains
the extemporaneous tone: he speaks excitedly, barely suggesting
the seriousness of his intention or the difficulty of his project. With
apparent unconcern he notes that his "present" is his "presence,"
thus glossing over Whitman's earnest reminder—"He who touches
this book touches a man"—while at the same time suggesting it.
Similarly, his statement of method—""No forms less/ than activity"—recalls Williams's "No ideas but in things!"; but it too is
swept along by the rushing lines. The rhythm almost grinds to a
halt, however, when the subject is love.

The love motif shapes the other major themes: what the hero
thinks about and writes about depends first and last on the lady
with the "opaque" face. This emphasis is introduced in *Pieces* by
the following four stanzas of "As real as thinking" which must be
read slowly. The concentration of dentates, plosives, and gutterals
in these lines convey a sense of anxious deliberation:

> Small facts
> of eyes, hair
> blonde, face
>
> looking like a
> flat painted
> board. How

opaque as if
a reflection
merely, skin

vague gloves of
randomly seen
colors.

Creeley's implict preoccupation throughout the romance involves the relationship between the hero and the lady with the
"opaque" face. His attitude toward the hero's frustrations and
disappointments can usefully be measured in terms of Zukofsky's
attitude toward love because in *Pieces* Zukofsky functions as the
wise, older poet who oversees the action. The connection between
Creeley's development of the love motif and his selection of a title
for his sequence is hinted at in his introduction to *A,* written in
1967 at the same time he started to write most of the poems for his
own sequence, which was published in 1969. It is not surprising
that his comments about Zukofsky's work tell us about his own. For
instance, under the aegis of a general introductory remark— "One
hears in the possibility another has articulated what may thus bring
clear one's own"[3]—Creeley cites the substance of the passage from
It Was quoted earlier in this chapter. He also notes that despite the
bitter complexities of Zukofsky's life he feels compelled to bring
the message to "angels and bastards interchangeably" that life
bears harmony to those wise enough to believe in "happy, im-
measurable love" (*A-12*). Zukofsky defined himself as a devotee
and apprentice of Bach, Mozart, and Shakespeare, who told "The
oldest story aching on love":

> But for your pages you tore up
> Of which I pasted the pieces
> How else may we prove together
> That the blindness of love was the eyes' refusal
> To see what they let get by.
>
> (*A-13*)

In *Pieces,* it is the hero's fate to rework "the pieces" and so
undertake Zukofsky's task. The question is whether or not he will
be able to say at the conclusion of the poem what Zukofsky found
himself saying at the conclusion of *It Was:* "—You were good to
me."

THE PERILOUS JOURNEY

The First Descent

The immediate rationale for the hero's first descent springs from his effort to penetrate the woman's "opaque" face and to find the "hand" beneath the "vague glove" referred to in "As real as thinking":

> Inside
> and out
>
> impossible
> locations—
>
> reaching in
> from out-
>
> side, out
> from in-
>
> side—as
> middle:
>
> one
> hand.
>   (p. 4)

At the same time that the hero is trying to establish a less superficial relationship with the woman, his "reaching in" to the "middle" also suggests a self-directed activity effected in his own imagination. It might be that the lonely hero hopes by turning inward to recover wisdom or satisfaction through self-analysis or perhaps through bodily consciousness. In either case, something important to the sequence is happening "inside" the speaker.

There is a link between this inner source of vitality and creative spirit. The epigraph for *Pieces* comes from Allen Ginsberg's poem "Song," and it, together with Creeley's interpretation of this passage, provides clues to the full meaning of the first descent:

```
yes, yes,
            that's what
I wanted,
            I always wanted,
I always wanted,
            to return
to the body
            where I was born.
```

In a brief critical note called "I'm given to write poems," Creeley explained that he found in Ginsberg's poem more than simply an invitation to sentient awareness: "It is, then to 'return' not to oneself as some egocentric center, but to experience oneself as *in* the world, thus, through this agency or fact we call, variously, 'poetry.' "[4] Creeley's explication of Ginsberg's poem centers on the relationship between the desire "to return/ to the body" and " 'poetry.' " Though Creeley does not make it plain in the first descent, the passage is implicitly an extension of the metaphor he discerns in "Song." Ginsberg's account of the function of language to "carry a purely subjective projection from the body" is instructive. He would "yoke the body to the search, the path that you're into" and arouse attention to that sense of inner space by defining language as a "magic spell"

> where any attempt at rational description is abandoned from the very beginning and it is understood that the language is purely magic spell and that its function is to be only magic spell, mantra, or prayer, so to speak—that its function is only to be a physiological vehicle for feelings and understood as such.[5]

The First Part

Having descended to the "middle," the hero describes (p. 5) what he observes. Mystifying contradictions—"no sun/ but sun—// or water/ but wetness found—" lead him to philosophize: "This life cannot be lived/ apart from what it must forgive." The pat sentiment and neat rhymes of his cracker-barrel wisdom suggest that his resigned outlook has not emerged from his own experience;

yet his final statement in *Pieces* resembles the idea expressed here.
In the seventy-six pages of text that come between, the hero
considers and reconsiders his experience from a wide variety of
angles. At the end of the sequence, his answer to the question
raised at the start—"What truth is it/ that makes men so
miserable?"—bears the mark of a seasoned observer.

The issue in *Pieces*, then, is what the hero "must forgive" if he is
to live. He begins by contemplating his ostensibly stable family
situation, the situation that is closest to him:

> The Family
>
> Father
> and mother
> and sister
> and sister
> and sister.
>
> .
>
> Here we are.
> There are five
> ways to say this.
>   (p. 5)

Nonetheless, he is restless. As the poem moves on, concrete details
taken from predictable everyday life are juxtaposed with his vague
feelings about them, feelings that hint at his uneasiness. For
instance, he interrupts his catalogue of the commonplace, including such clinical reports as "Cup./ Bowl./ Saucer./ Full." and
"The door, the hat,/ the chair, the fact" (p. 7) with half-said
reservations about their significance:

> Having to—
>
> Having to—
> what do I think
> to say now.
>
> Nothing but
> comes and goes.
> in a moment.
>   (p. 6)

In "Pieces of cake" the tension between the hero's contented
acceptance of "small facts" and his tentative rejection of them
reaches fuller expression:

> Pieces of cake
> Pieces of cake crumbling
> in the hand trying to hold
> them together to give each
> of the seated guests a piece.
>
>
> Willow, the house, an egg—
> what do they make?
>
> Hat, happy, a door—
> what more.
>> (p. 8)

The congenial host, while trying "to give each/ of the seated guests a piece," questions the significance of these pieces of cake as well as of his gesture. This unremarkable combination of impulses becomes, in the context that follows, the basis for disturbing confusions.

The scene shifts abruptly from this homely circumstance to a supernatural world in which the hero speculates about "what more" there is to his ordinary life. In an important poem called "The Finger," the hero of *Pieces* learns that he is the agent for an eternal poetic essence. He is told by mysterious powers that his "fate would be timeless," his burden will be the perpetual retelling of his own story:

> . . . . Again
>
> and again I was to
> get it right, the story I
> myself knew only the way of,
> but the purpose if it
>
> had one, was not mine.
>> (p. 9)

The idea that the hero is destined to tell the story he alone knows in behalf of a mysterious power is in keeping with Creeley's thoughts about the creative process as he explains them in several essays. In one of them, for instance, he describes Robert Graves's *The White Goddess* as a book "much concerned with the image of how poets have worked in this world, and of the 'magic' source by which they have survived." He goes on to say that "if you are a poet, you will know that presence of fate" and he explains to the reader:

> The obedience of a poet's gratitude, for this, is the authority which you hear in his poems, and it is obedience to a presence which is, if you will, that which is not understood, ever; but which he characterizes as all that can happen in living, and seeks to form an emblem for, with words.[6]

Although Creeley does not subscribe to the systematization of such an "authority" as Graves outlines it in *The White Goddess,* he does recognize the awesome "presence of fate" that compels a poet to write and enables him to endure. In *Pieces,* it is the hero's "obedience" to this "authority" that causes him to subordinate his personal frustrations to his fate of carrying out his mission.

In a sacred and primordial place reminiscent of Duncan's "eternal pasture"—a place, Creeley says in a critical note, "poetry not only creates but itself issues from"[7]—the hero receives his mission: "The quiet shatter of the light,/ the image folded into/ endlessly opening patterns—." The emphasis in "The Finger" is not on the place itself but on the hero's attempt to understand what is expected of him and how he can best execute his responsibility.

First he wonders about the mysterious powers who are associated with this place: "had they faced me into/ the light so that my/ eye was blinded?" Then he questions the limits of his endurance—"To go on telling the story,/to go on though no one hears it,/ to the end of my days?"—and his ability: "is that right, have I said it—." As "The Finger" continues, it becomes clear that the hero wants the reassurance of others; and it becomes equally clear that no one will help him. Those who told him his "fate would be timeless" are "gone." He searches in vain for Aphrodite, for the pureness of her beauty he "had known of,/ and caught sight of as *maid*—." He knew Athena "perhaps even more" but there is no contact between them although,

> . . . . She was there
> in the room's corner, as she would be,
> bent by a wind it seemed

would never stop blowing,
braced like a seabird,
with those endlessly clear gray eyes.
. . . . (pp. 9–10)

Athena is felt to have a special function in the room of "blinding
light." Her "endlessly clear grey eyes" promise knowledge; yet she
does not reveal it. In similar fashion, Hermes remains deliberately
aloof. Traditionally, Hermes, the god of healing, is the mediator
between the human mind and divine wisdom. But when in this
poem the hero tries to talk to him, his face, made more inscrutable
by "dark glasses," merely reflects the fated hero's "cast of words."
With no one to turn to, he is left to sustain himself with his own
determination inspired by the mysterious "authority":

And the power to tell
is glory. One unto one
unto one. And though all
mistake it, it is one.
(p. 10)

The scene in "The Finger" shifts to a dusty place of "scattered
pieces" and the hero tries to tell his story to the sensual woman he
finds there. Unlike Aphrodite, who impressed the hero with her
"girlish openness," this woman suggests the demonic. At first the
emphasis is on her skin—""so warm,/ so massive"—as she lounges
"before the fire and its heat"; but the focus quickly centers on her
lustfulness:

She laughed and turned
and the heavy folds of cloth

parted. The nakedness
burned. Her heavy breath,
her ugliness, her lust—
but her laughing, her low

chuckling laugh, the way
she moved her hand to the
naked breast, then to
her belly, her hand with its fingers.
(p. 12)

The woman, like Aphrodite, is remote—"To approach, to hold

her,/ was not possible"—and, like Athena, holds the key to wisdom—she "smiled/ in some deepening knowledge" and "her eyes" were "the depth of all one had thought of,/ again and again and again." Yet she reveals nothing although the hero makes several attempts to engage her attention.

His "whistled,/ insistent song," an image for the delightful "wonder" he proposes to create, does not "move her"; his effort to "jiggle a world before her/ made of his mind," a more specific reference to the wondrous "sentence" composed of thought, is met with her "half-sleepy" indulgence; finally, his offered promise—

> Listen to me, let
> me touch you
> there. You are young again,
> and you are looking at me.
> (p. 13)

—is greeted with indifference: "She was laughing, she was/ laughing, at me."

Taken together, the lustful woman, Aphrodite, and Athena represent all women. "It's an absolute manifestation throughout all realms of existence in the woman figure," Creeley has said of this poem in an interview.[8] In "The Finger" itself, the hero suggests her composite nature by attesting to his own confusions—"Is she that woman,/ or this one"—and by describing her in all-inclusive terms:

> She was young,
> she was old,
> she was small.
> She was tall with
>
> extraordinary grace.
> (p. 12)

Similarly, the hero is portrayed in various guises of man. At first, he is "a stranger,// bearded, with clothes that were/ old and torn." This and the fact that one of the first phrases in "The Finger" is "*So that*" suggest Creeley is picking up where Pound left off in Canto I and presenting the hero as an Odysseus figure. The hero might be a Hephaestus figure because he is abandoned by the mysterious powers and linked with Aphrodite. Or perhaps he might be a Tiresias figure, because of the mention of his possible blindness and because his sexual identity is at one point undefined: he "was neither a man nor not one."

The hero is thus associated with several mythological figures and the implication is that he might be or at least would like to be one of them. Of the various identities he might assume, the one possibility that is carried forward in the sequence involves his relationship with Athena and Hermes. Athena and Hermes helped Perseus kill the Gorgon Medusa he saw reflected in his shield, and rescue the fascinating princess Andromeda. The hero's futile attempt to kill the sea monster who "devoured us all" and his realization that his wife seen "in the mirror" is "patent, pathetic, insured" suggests he is following Perseus's course of action. That he fails ultimately is foretold here because Athena and Hermes refuse to help him.

In addition to the several mythological references in "The Finger," there are other supernatural components as well which bring with them the sense of the hero's involvement in a large and impersonal context. In another section of the poem, the hero seems to be in touch with some aspect of the collective unconscious experience: "I'll dance a jig I learned/ long before we were born" (p. 10). In still another section of the poem (p. 10), he is associated with Christ: "I saw the stones thrown/ at her, I felt a radiance transform/ my hands and my face./ I blessed her, I was one." And, too, he is an innocent "manny" (a coined word) who wants to know about the erotic woman lounging by the fire and how he might keep her attention. Creeley's presentation of the man and woman, each as "an absolute manifestation throughout all realms of existence," underscores the timeless nature of the significance and the difficulty bound up with the hero's mission.

It is clear that the hero is unable to communicate his story in a persuasive fashion. Despite his increasing anxiety about his problem, when he meets the "Gemini" (p. 15) he manages to tell them that he brings "sequences// of words that are not to be understood/ but somehow given to a world." Ideally, the Gemini should be able to sympathize and be eager to help because, traditionally, they are advisers to man. Moreover, they are "confined to a place ruled// by a moon" and the idea that "if the// moon rules, there is/ 'domestic harmony'" has something to do with the purpose of his story. Yet they cannot grasp his meaning. Their confusion is particularly disappointing to the hero because of his stated strategy: "From one to two,/ is the first rule." Since "of two minds the twin/ is to double life given," they are theoretically in an excellent position to clarify the difficulties involved. But their "fight// to possess" the hero's words ends in a quarrel. The self-pitying hero is left alone, sardonically castigating himself: "Hence the fool dances/ in endless happiness." Nonetheless he recovers his composure, restates his message—

> Where it is
> was and
> will be never
> only here.

(p. 17)

—and accepts the challenge of finding a better way to deliver it.

The Second Descent

> —fluttering as
> falling, leaves,
> knives, to
> avoid—tunnel
> down the
> vague sides . . .
>
>
>   .
>
>
> —it
> it—

(p. 17)

The hero's second descent is a more dangerous experience than his first; it involves "knives" to be avoided and a "tunnel" with "vague sides," whereas his first descent involved only awkward "impossible/ locations" and the "middle" of his own being (p. 4). The key phrase "tunnel/ down" with its sexual overtones serves to comment on the complex nature of his present ordeal. It is, first of all, a simple description of the threatening activity in progress which hints at the possibility of castration, but it can also be interpreted as a command from the mysterious powers who singled out the hero as their agent. The image of the helpless hero"—fluttering as/ falling, leaves" supports the suggestion that an impersonal, manipulative force is actively present.

Although the "descent" passage implies his obedience to a demanding authority, whether it is the woman with the "opaque" face or the creative spirit, the emphasis here is on the risk he assumes. The visual image of the hero falling through a "tunnel" of "knives" measures the extent to which he will go in an effort to tell his own story at the same time that it focuses attention on the hazards inherent in "—it/ it—."

The Second Part

In the opening stanzas of *Pieces*, the hero was confident. He described himself as a poet, his "present" as "a sentence/ which// began it *was*" and which, quite casually, would say "something/ as it goes." Later he referred to himself as a host, his gift as "pieces of cake." Though the "cake" crumbled in his hand when he tried "to give each/ of the seated guests a piece," he was relaxed. When he failed to explain " 'domestic harmony' " to the Gemini, he was despondent. Here, at the beginning of the second part of his perilous journey, his voice is harsh, and his mood is desperate. He defines himself as the " 'Drinking Gourd' " and asks the reader to " 'follow' " him. Again he will offer the gift, as is his obligation, though his previous failures to communicate have taken a toll. His tensely put, insistent, self-addressed directive attests to his present sense of urgency:

> *Present again*
> *present present*
> *again present*
> *present again.*
> (p. 17)

Ironically, the hero's treacherous descent to "—it/ it—" does not bring him into a mysterious world of supernatural figures; rather, it brings him into the recognizable everyday world of "small facts." The lines that preface his actual journey provoke an eerie impression: "Leaves falling,/ knives, a windspout/ of nostalgic faces,/ into the air." The words—"leaves," "falling," and "knives" —connect back to his dangerous descent and move the story forward by suggesting the strange atmosphere of the place in which the ensuing action will occur. The action itself has to do with the hero's thoughts and feelings as he drives from Bloomington, Indiana, to Lexington, Kentucky.

Preoccupied with his "present," he relates what he sees on the road to his need to tell his story. For instance, "the trucks/ in front with/ the unseen drivers" cause him to remember nicknames, "Stony Lonesome. Gnaw-/ bone." These names evoke relevant memories of army experience:

> *A Christmas*
> *present—all*
> *present and ac-*
> *counted for? Sir?*
> (p. 18)

This in turn leads him to speculate about the uncertain fate of presents: "The 'present dented,'/ call it 'long/ distance.'" He wonders if perhaps he will be able to deliver the gift after all.

At the same time that the hero doubts his artistic ability, he questions the value of his present. The message apparently has to do with the celebration of "here"; yet he is vaguely dissatisfied with his trip and asks, "Where in/ the world then an-/ other place?" The message presumably has to do with harmony, with taking place in "that sun of/*a universe of mine*"; but he seems bored by the monotony of his experience, represented by the "exceptionally smooth/ and even surface" of the road. The message seemingly has to do with the creation of wonders "All in the mind"; however, he questions how the fact that he spent "twenty eight/ dollars" to rent the car he is driving could in any way inspire a fascinating thought.

The polarity between his dissatisfaction with the actual "here" of "small facts" and his growing interest in the possibility of a more meaningful "there" will become a major source of tension in *Pieces.* At this point in the sequence, the issue is held in abeyance while the hero attends to his responsibility. Although he urges himself to meet his obligation squarely—"*Go on. Tell*/ *me, them, him,*/ *her, their*/ apparent forms" (pp. 18–19)—he cannot reconcile his conflicting feelings easily. At last, he turns to the reader for advice:

> . . . . Give
> me a present, your
> hand to help
>
> me understand this.
> So far, so long,
> so anywhere a
> place if not this
>
> one—

                    (pp. 19–20)

Encouraged, he is "screaming a lovely/ song" about freedom triumphing over oppression, a "song" analogous to his hopeful message about "harmony." Yet perhaps in response to his most recent futile effort—his hope to enlighten the Gemini on " 'domestic harmony' "—he feels his relationship with the reader is tenuous. The final lines of "FOLLOW THE DRINKING GOURD . . ." show him wondering if his attempt to communicate was "*right* or/ *wrong*," and deciding to "wander on."

The reason for the hero's distress is twofold. An emphatic distinction must now be made between his role as a poet, obedient to a mysterious authority, and his personal thoughts and feelings. In his capacity as a poet, he is unable to state the message he is fated to deliver in an effective way. What is becoming increasingly clear is that his personal problems are the cause of his professional ones. Having tested the idea—the literal world of "small facts" is all there is—against his own experience, imaged as the story he alone knows "the way of," he finds that he cannot accept this idea as a reassurance worth proposing. This personal reluctance to celebrate the "here" of "small facts" seems to derive from his antipathy toward his wife.

"The Moon," the poem that follows in the text, contrasts the banality of his marriage with the "lovely// bright clarity" of the moon. The full impact of the poem depends on the reader remembering "The Family," an earlier, thematically similar poem in *Pieces* that hinted at the cause of the hero's restlessness, and "Gemini," a poem in which the moon represented "domestic harmony":

The Moon

Earlier in the evening the moon
was clear to the east,
over the snow of the yard
and fields—a lovely

bright clarity and perfect
roundness, isolate,
riding as they say the
black sky. Then we went

about our businesses of the
evening, eating supper, talking,
watching television, then
going to bed, making love,

and then to sleep. But before
we did I asked her to look
out the window at the moon
now straight up, so that

she bent her head and looked
sharply up, to see it.
Through the night it must
have shone on, in that

fact of things—another
moon, another night—a
full moon in the winter's
space, a white loneliness.

I came awake to the blue
white light in the darkness,
and felt as if someone
were there, waiting, alone.

(pp. 20–21)

Apostrophizing the moon, the hero uses a sexual image. He describes it "riding" the "black sky" with a sweeping sense of freedom though its actual course is rigidly prescribed. It is "isolate" and "perfect": nothing else seems needed. In contrast, the lonely hero is unsatisfied, as the series of mechanically repetitive participial phrases in the third stanza of "The Moon" make plain; his marriage is tedious, businesslike, and restrictive. The dramatic center of the poem—"I asked her to look/ out the window at the moon"—ends with an anticlimax: although she willingly follows his directive, she is unable to grasp his meaning. The implication is that his effectiveness as a poet is being compromised by the frustrating nature of his marriage. In the concluding lines of "The Moon," the hero "felt as if someone/ were there, waiting, alone." "Someone" might represent the person for whom his message is intended—the person for whom the "purpose" of his story will make sense, the person who would welcome words of reassurance.

Every major poem in *Pieces* thus far has ended with the hero's realization that as a poet, he has failed to execute his responsibility. On each occasion, he rededicates himself to his task and explores another aspect of his experience he hopes will illustrate his message about "harmony." Yet each time, ironically, his contemplation of the "small facts" of his life contradicts his intention; he scans the ordinary "here" and finds that he is lonely and bored, a literal situation that he, personally, neither can explain away nor happily accept.

The difference between the tedious "here" and the possibility of a satisfying "there" is a more pressing concern in "Numbers," a long sequence of poems which constitutes a major portion of the second part of his adventurous journey. The hero uses his mathematical imagination as a focal point. Apart from its subject—various loosely connected thoughts and feelings about the numbers one through nine and then zero—"Numbers" is unified by issues involving love, poetry, and thought which recur throughout the sequence. The emphasis in these poems is on the nature of thought; what is called into question is the difference between the actually immediate event and what the mind makes of it, that "point of so-called/ consciousness [which] is forever/ a word making up/ this world of more/ or less than it is" (p. 23).

On the one hand, the hero directs attention to the literal reality:

> This time, this
> place, this
> one.
>   (from "One," p. 22)

> Look
> at
> the
> light
> of
> this
> hour.
>   (from "<u>Seven</u>," p. 28)

On the other hand, he indulges his tendency to assign profound importance to everyday details. The number four becomes an arbitrary symbol for "enduring experience"; "six" signifies holiness:

> The card which is the
> four of hearts must
> mean enduring experience
> of life. What other
> meaning could it have.
>   (from "<u>Four</u>," p. 25)

> on the sixth
> day had finished
> all creation—
>
> hence holy—
>   (from "<u>Six</u>," p. 27)

The numbers four and six stimulate the hero's imagination. His thoughts play over them, investing their neutral reality with wondrous possibilities, which in turn can be contemplated, questioned, and qualified. The intellectual exercise relieves the tediousness of his everyday experience made up of "small facts," but it is not a substitute for it. His abstract thinking about "four" is tempered by his commitment to reality: "Is a door/ four—but/ who enters." "Six" may represent holiness, but it may represent a scientific fact as well: "the sun/ is 'furthest from// equator & appears/ to pause, before/ returning . . .' "

Perhaps the central cause of the hero's dissatisfaction with the "small facts" of his life has to do with his painful awareness that he is essentially alone. He is tempted to mitigate this feeling of loneliness, a crucial aspect of the love motif, by ignoring the actual and contriving a world in his own mind instead. Using the number one as his point of reference, he states his problem and his proposed solution:

> Don't leave me
> Love me. One by one.
>
> As if to sit
> by me were another
> who did sit. So
>
> to make you
> mine, in the mind,
> to know you.
> (from "<u>Two</u>," p. 23)

A confrontation is building between the hero's personal situation and his professional responsibility. He is given to infuse "small facts" with transcendent meaning in such a way that he can derive a sense of belonging in the world from his humdrum experience. But he is fated to convey the message that "small facts," in themselves, are sufficient evidence of harmony. Although he often uses his thoughts and feelings about numbers to express his personal insights, many of his observations about numbers are intended to illustrate the ordained purpose of his story.

He notes that each number is a distinct entity; yet each is related to another so that taken together they constitute a harmonious whole. For instance, "five" can be thought of in terms of other numbers:

> . . . Somehow the extra
> one—what is more than four—
>
> reassured me there would be
> enough. Twos and threes or
> one and four is plenty.
> (from "<u>Five</u>," p. 27)

"Five," however has its own individual function: "A way to draw stars." Similarly, "eight" reminds him that "two fours/ show the way," but "eight" also has its own unique quality:

Oct-
ag-
on-
al.
        (from "Eight," p. 31)

Each number, then, has its own particular function; but it is,
simultaneously, an integral part of a numerical scheme.

The hero feels it might be possible to learn about harmony from
numbers, a lesson his intuition tells him he needs to learn if he is to
feel at home with himself and at home in the world. When he gets
to "nine," a " 'triply sacred and perfect/ number,' " he asks:
"that// resolves what—/ in the shifting,/ fading containment?" He
will learn nothing from even the "sacred" number nine (as before
he learned nothing from the mysterious powers who told him his
"fate would be timeless" [p. 9]). The end result of his contemplation makes his disappointment plain.

What law
or
mystery

is involved
protects
itself.
        (from "Nine," p. 33)

The conflict between the hero's impulse to ignore the prosaic
"small fact" because he can learn nothing of its intrinsic mystery or
its precise place in the universal whole, and his obligation to
celebrate the "here," culminate in the poem given over to the final
number, "zero," a number personified by the fool. Although the
fool is described as a separate character, it is helpful to consider
him a dramatization of that part of the hero's personality which
refuses to accept "here" as all there is. In the poem "Zero," the
fools' solipsistic viewpoint is set down:

There is no trick to reality—
        a mind
makes it, any
        mind. You

walk the years in a
    nothing, a no
place I know as well as
    the last breath

I took, blowing the smoke
    out of a mouth
will also go nowhere,
    having found its way.
                    (from "Zero," pp. 33–34)

The fool himself is described in a long prose passage which is a
quotation from Arthur Waite's *Pictorial Key to the Tarot*, a
passage Creeley speaks of in an interview as "a beautiful estimate
of the experience of nothing."[9] In this satiric character sketch, he is
presented as a young man in "gorgeous vestments" who "surveys"
the "expanse of sky rather than the prospect below." Standing at
the edge of an abyss, he is supremely confident: "it is as if angels
were waiting to uphold him." His face is "full of intelligence and
expectant dream." He is like "a prince of the other world on his
travels through this one," a prince associated with the sun which
"knows whence he came, whither he is going, and how he will
return by another path after many days."

At this point the hero, who—in contrast to the fool—has been
described as an apprehensive stranger in tattered clothes, associated with the moon, and abandoned by the mysterious powers,
rivets his attention on the bedpost. He considers its "extraordinary
shape," and goes on to compare it with the familiar "cross bar of
the collar/ bone." His thoughts have nothing to do with exotic
adventures; rather, he broods over the demands of an insistent
woman: "What she says she wants/ she wants she says."

The hero and the fool are diametrically opposed to each other
because of their preoccupations, a contrast further suggested by
their markedly different appearances. An important purpose of the
hero's story, however, is to illuminate the idea that contradictory
impulses and conflicting opinions can coexist in the world. A key
passage at this point—

One/ the Sun/
Moon/ one.
            (p. 36)

—foreshadows the ultimate reconciliation between the hero's alternative selves, or, if you will, the hero and the fool.

Although the hero seems confused at the moment, he warns the reader not to dismiss him:

> The pen,
> the lines it
> leaves, forms
> divine—nor
> laugh nor giggle.
> This prescription
> is true.
> Truth is a scrawl
> all told
> in all.
>
> (p. 36)

He reminds us that he is on a divinely ordained mission, and that he has endured danger ("leaves" recalls the "tunnel" of "knives") in his effort to make the true remedy ("prescription") clear. That communication is difficult is his rationalization, because he has promised to tell "all," though by admitting his hesitations and mistakes he makes himself vulnerable ("laugh" and "giggle" bring to mind the amused response of the lustful woman lounging before the fire). In sum, "Numbers" ends on an ingratiating note. The hero has reestablished himself as the emissary of mysterious powers. He will go on in the hope that the "truth" will emerge from the mélange of confusions that mark his own diverse experience, the elements that constitute the story he alone knows "the way of" (p. 9).

The Third Descent

The hero's descent to "Chicago" is a punishing, emotional ordeal by virtue of which the vulnerable though willing sufferer hopes to complete his assigned task. In "Names," just preceding "Chicago," he speaks in behalf of actual people who seem to be close by, as well as for mysterious powers he met in the mythological past: Harry, Miriam, Peter, Robert, John, William, Tom, Helen, Ethel, and "that woman whose name/ he can't remember" charge him "to tell/ all they know." By implication, the hero is feeling

pressured either to satisfy their collective expectations or to explain
to the group why he has failed.

The burdened hero seems forced by his anxiety to acknowledge
that he is tense, that he is barely able to maintain his composure:
"Can feel it in the pushing,/ not letting myself relax/ for any
reason, hanging on." As suggested by the abrupt lines that follow,
he is worrying about the complexities bound up with the possibility
of thinking in a relaxed manner, a prized activity essential to his
creation of a wondrous sentence made up of his random thoughts:

> Thinking—and coincident
> experience of the situation.
>
> "I think he'll hit me."
> He does. Etc.
>
> •
>
> Reflector/ -ive/ -ed.
>   (p. 38)

The desperate atmosphere in which his third descent occurs
derives from his reluctant understanding that his intellectual
indecisiveness has distressing ramifications, that both real people
and supernatural beings are making demands upon him, and that
he is losing control of his now volatile feelings. Impelled by his
determination to meet his responsibilities, the hero goes to the
hell-town of Chicago:

> Chicago
> Say that you're
>   lonely—and want
> something to
>   place you—
>
> going around groping
>   either by mind
> or hand—but behind
>   the pun is a
>
> door you keep open,
>   one way,
> so they won't touch you
>   and still let you stay.

.

I can't see in
    this place more
than the walls
    and door—
a light flat
    and air hot,
and drab, drab, drab
    and locked.

———————————

Would dying be here?
Never go anywhere you
    can't live.

———————————

(pp. 38–39)

The familiar imagery identifying the hero's physical handicap—he sees a "light" which appears "flat"—emphasizes the fact
that he has suffered earlier trials. The reader is thus reminded that
the character who is now trapped in the hot, drab room is the same
character who, at the start of *Pieces,* saw a face he described as
"looking like a/ flat painted board" and who, on the road from
Indiana to Kentucky, surveyed "a flat-/ seeming distance." His
ordeal has been long and painful; he might be approaching the
limit of his endurance, a possibility he has feared throughout the
sequence.

With the press of time and the loss of energy, ordering factors in
the third part of his adventure, the hero will race from one subject
to the next, often contradicting himself and often breaking off in
the middle of a thought. We can sympathize with his frantic
behavior because we are reminded from time to time that he has
genuine cause to feel unnerved. For instance, toward the end of
this part of his perilous journey, he will be described in terms
recalling his terrifying descent to Chicago. Anxiety-stricken he
will be:

> Like a man committed to searching
> out long darkened corridors with doors,
> and only the spot of the flashlight to
> be a way into and back out, to safety.
>   (p. 60)

The poetic purpose of this flashback, like the effect gained by mentioning his compromised sight, is first to insist on the hero's tenacity, long and sorely tried, and then to suggest that the reader lend him support in consideration of his weakened state.

The Third Part

Against the backdrop of hellish city life, the hero tries to make sense of his depressingly banal experience and, as the plural voice suggests, our own: "Where we are there must/ be something to place us" (p. 64). As our representative, he is first locked in an "institutional" noisy room of "shrinking space" in Chicago, and then trapped by the "rectangular enclosures" of New York, where he feels a "continual sense of small," a feeling intensified by the cold and rain. Rescued by Allen (presumably Allen Ginsberg), with whom he travels cross-country by plane, he reflects on the impersonalization created by city life. He speculates that his distorted perceptions are both symptom and cause of an illness that afflicts the word:

> Allen's saying as we fly out of NYC—the look of the city underneath us like a cellular growth, "cancer"—so that senses of men on the earth as an investment of it radiates a world cancer—Burroughs' "law" finally quite clear. (p. 49)

Though he seems overwhelmed by the horrors of city life and though he has no specific remedy to offer, he can point out the source of the disease: people forget that "The *world*" (from "They," p. 47) is where they live, and thus they have a personal, vested interest as well as a responsibility to clean it up. A commitment to a human orientation will necessarily involve rethinking entrenched attitudes; yet many would scramble for more of the same and thus perpetuate the status quo: "Take advantage of this,/ take advantage of what's downtown/ and link the two with a/ rapid transit system . . ." (p. 64) while ignoring urgent human issues, such as the confrontation building between "unresponsible people" and "serious people" in New Brunswick over "the language/ of instruction/ for their children . . ." ("The News," pp. 62–63). Some get caught up in bombastic, political rhetoric:

> Canada
>
> "The maple leaf forever"
>   "in 1867—"
> "inspired the world
>   to say—"
>
> (p. 45)

Others are easily distracted by the more sensational, for instance "a giggly ode about/ motherfuckers." In general, a crisis exists in America—"Give back// what we are, these people you made,/ *us,* and nowhere but you to be" (p. 42)—but those with "little voices" are explicitly hostile to change and would prefer

> The grand time when the words
> were fit for human allegation,
>
> and imagination of small, local
> containments, and the lids fit.
>
> (p. 41)

The hero thus finds himself in an impersonal society where people are unwilling to be of genuine use either to each other or, in a basic sense, to themselves. His personal relationships are equally disappointing; a friend he would like to help patronizes him; another glibly analyzes his "trouble." Although his situation is not completely dismal—Allen encourages him to recognize an experience as the "possibility of pleasure" (p. 55) and the Curleys he recalls with affection—the cumulative effect of his comments about people he knows underscores his loneliness.

Of the hero's various frustrating relationships, his empty relationship with the lady with the "opaque" face was felt to be the crucial one from the start of *Pieces.* At this point in the sequence, he returns to San Francisco where he eagerly anticipates their reunion: "The sun makes spring now,// a renewal possibly of like energy,/ something forgotten almost remembered,/ echoes in my mind like the grass" (p. 51). We do not, however, get a poem that celebrates love; rather, we get a poem that focuses on separateness:

> Your opaqueness, at moments,
> would be the mirror. Your
> face closed as a door—
>
> that insists on nothing,
> but not to be entered—
> wanting simply to be left alone.
>
> I slept, it seemed, the moment
> I lay down in the bed, even,
> it might have been, impatient
>
> to be out of it, gone away,
> to what densities can be there
> in a night's sleep, day by day
>
> But, all in the mind it comes
> and goes. My own life is given
> me back again, something forgotten.
>   (p. 51)

This section of "No clouds" either can be read simply as a poem about a credible human relationship between husband and wife, or it can be read as a mythological poem. That is, this recognizably human woman, who by her indifference disappoints the hero, might also be a contemporary version of a Medusa figure. That her face "would be the mirror," and that the hero falls asleep immediately after looking at her, suggest she is.

The mythological story that was introduced in "The Finger" and that now and again appears throughout *Pieces* seems to be the inverse of the Perseus legend. Whereas Perseus was helped by Athena and Hermes, the hero of this sequence is abandoned by them. Thus his inability to prevail over the woman with the "opaque" face is not surprising. It might be that the woman with the remarkable face who fails the hero is the counterpart to one of the Graeae, Medusa's sisters. An essential part of Perseus's strategy to kill Medusa involved taking magic weapons and disguises from the Graeae: winged sandals that enabled him to fly, a curved knife to decapitate Medusa, a bag in which to conceal her head, and a helmet that made him invisible. By contrast, in the poems of the third part of the perilous journey that follow "No clouds," the hero "gets there" by means of his "head I do put wheels on,/ and two arms and two legs" (p. 60). He is pictured in a home movie with "the echoic scissors" for "cutting hair off" (p. 56) and, instead of carrying a sack, he is "unwrapping/ the floor covering and rolling it/ forward" (p. 65). Finally, he is completely visible, "on—the/ light bulb// overhead" (p. 53). Though these details fit into the human story the wondrous "sentence" of *Pieces* tells, they also have a place in the mythological story that is interspersed throughout the sequence.

Whether the poem "No clouds" is read for its mythological or its human implications, the central point is that in either case the hero, thrown back on his inner resources after meeting the impenetrable woman, takes refuge in his imagination. This development in the love motif affects the way he thinks:

> But, all in the mind it comes
> and goes. My own life is given
> me back again, something forgotten.
>
> (p. 51)

On the one hand, his "situation of feeling increasingly 'apart' " (p. 53) leads him to wonder, with greater poignancy than expressed before in *Pieces*, if "there might be/ an imaginary/ place to be—/ there might be" (pp. 58–59). His tendency to reject the idea that "a life/ is nothing more than itself" (p. 48), and to explore the possibility "if what might be might be,/ if what has to be is otherwise" (p. 57) derives from his need to escape "obvious unrest and frustration":

> Thinking—a tacit, tactile distance between us at this moment —much as if we had lives in "different worlds"—which, I suppose, would be the case despite all closeness otherwise, i.e., almost as if the moment one were "thinking," and not literally taking, finding place in something we both had occasion in, that this fact of things becomes a separation. I.e., it seems not possible to live the "same" life, no matter what one wants, wills, or tries to have the so-called "case."—Like old "romantic" self-query, come of obvious unrest and frustration. (p. 52)

On the other hand, he knows if he carries this activity of " 'thinking,' and not literally taking, finding place" to an extreme, he may lose sight of literal reality altogether. In tense, brittle lines, he reminds himself that" 'here,' as a habit, is what we are lacking *here*" (p. 56), that there is no meaningful escape from the living present:

> Nowhere one
> goes will
> one ever
> be away
> enough from
> wherever
> one was.
> > (p. 50)

He senses intuitively that he must somehow come to terms with his lonely singleness:

> This singleness
> you make an evidence
> has purpose.
>
> You are not alone,
> however one—not
> so alone.
>
> Light finds a place
> you can see it in
> such singleness.
> > (p. 58)

By the close of the third part of the perilous journey, the hero realized that thinking, taken as a self-generating exercise, mocks his hope to understand. It becomes the subject of parody: "Each moment constitutes reality,/ or rather may constitute/ reality, or may have *done* so,/ or perhaps *will*?" (p. 62). Instead of allowing himself to get bogged down in a tangle of philsophical speculations, he must face his dilemma squarely: "In my own ego structure, have to find *place* for shift in imagination of experience" (p. 66), a shift that must take into account his awareness that he is essentially alone and his hope to be part of another's life. His note to his unresponsive wife ends with his plea "One wants *one*.// 'Love, Bob' " (p. 66).

Whatever the outcome, the hero's various confusions make up his story, a story he must tell if his fate is to be timeless (see "The Finger"). Though he takes the matter of his fate most seriously and thus often complains about being misunderstood, he has managed to remain a remarkably congenial storyteller. Here, his sustained, angry outburst directed at the reader serves to measure the intensity of his frustration and the seriousness of his effort:

> You want
>
> the fact
>
> of things
>
> in words,
>
> of words.
>
> .
>
> Endless trouble, endless pleasure,
> endless distance, endless ways.
>
> .
>
> What do you want with the phone
> if you won't answer it.
>
> .
>
> Don't say it doesn't rhyme
> if you won't read it—nor break the
>
> line in pieces that goes
> and goes and goes
>
> (pp. 61–62)

One of the major poetic achievements of *Pieces* has to do with the fact that the hero demands the reader's attention continuously, either by appealing to our good nature as he did before or by upbraiding us for our stupidity as he does now. *Pieces* argues that poetry is a shared experience which depends on the reader's active participation. It is not so much that the hero lectures us on the "fact/ of things" he understands better than we do; rather, it is that he presents these facts as he observes them and asks that we help fit them into a coherent pattern.

One of the facts he must deal with involves his disgust with the " 'breathtaking banalities' " (p. 41) of his life. Another fact, however, involves his affectionate impulses:

> Happy love, this
> agreement, coincidence
> like crossing streets.
>> (p. 45)

Later, he proclaims:

> Peace, brother, to all of it,
> in all senses, in all places,
> in every way, in all
> senses, in all places, in
> every way.
>> (p. 60)

Whether or not he can find personal comfort in these reassuring ideas of "happy love" and "peace" is one issue, and whether or not these ideas have something to do with the purpose of his story is another. He tries to define these matters more precisely by recalling the circumstance in which he was told that his "fate would be timeless" (p. 9) if he told the story he alone knew.

In the two poems following "Happy love"—"The Boy" and "3 in 1"—he reestablishes the mood of "The Finger" and reminds us of the content of the earlier poem as well. First, in "The Boy," the element of perversion connected with "the birth// of love" perhaps sets in motion memories of the hero's futile effort to approach the lustful woman. Similarly, another detail—the boy "grew a beard henceforth"—perhaps reminds us that the hero was presented as a "bearded stranger" at the opening of "The Finger." These fragile echoes gain strength in "3 in 1":

> 3 in 1
>
> The bird
> flies
> out the
> window. She
> flies.

.

The bird flies
out the
window. She
flies.

.

The bird
flies. She
flies.

(pp. 46–47)

In "The Finger," Athena was "braced like a seabird" in "the room's corner." In the poem at hand, the bird might be the owl, the providential bird associated with the wise Athena, or a symbol of Athena herself, its flight signaling the coming of knowledge. There are enough backward glances in "The Boy" and "3 in 1" to "The Finger" to suggest that the poem which follows them, entitled "They," should be interpreted as an extension of the hero's initial attempt to understand the mysterious powers who tempted him with a timeless fate if he told his story, but who refused to reveal its purpose. In "The Finger," "they" left him alone in an eternal hall of blinding light to find out for himself how he best might deliver the message.

In the poem "They," the hero resumes his speculations. He now thinks that he knew as much as "they" did at the time; he wonders if "they" might have been his own "imagination":

They

what could
they give me I
hadn't myself
discovered—

The *world,*—that
I'd fallen upon
in some
distracted drunkenness—

Or that the rules
were *wrong,* an
observation they
as well as I
knew now—

> *They* were imagination
> also. If they
> would be as the
> mind could see *them,*
>
> then it all was
> true and the
> mind followed and
> *I* also.
>
> (p. 47)

Because "the rules/ were *wrong,*" it was the hero's obligation to make it clear to the world "that if the// moon rules, there is/ 'domestic harmony' " ("Gemini," p. 16). Consequently, he used his response to the numbers one through nine and then zero as evidence in his debate between accepting his responsibility to give to the world a message that was fated to be misunderstood, and ignoring the difficult task, between accepting the literal "here" of "small facts," and yielding to the tantalizing possibility of intellectually creating a more satisfying "there," and, finally, between accepting the purpose of his "singleness" on faith, and demanding proof that he had a "place" in the "harmony" represented by numbers. Although he decided to carry out his destined mission—to bring "sequences// of words that are not to be understood/ but somehow given to a world" ("Gemini," p. 15)—he concluded he was unable to resolve the conflicts at issue: *"What law/ or/ mystery// is involved/ protects/ itself"* ("Nine," p. 33).

At the close of the third part of his perilous journey, the hero is once again on the verge of discovery. The seasonal imagery supports this sense of expectation. Up until this point in *Pieces,* references to the time of the year have been casual, almost unobtrusive. Yet his trip from Indiana to Kentucky did take place during the fall ("leaves, falling") and his descent into the dark room in Chicago was associated with the winter's cold. When he returned to his wife in San Francisco, "the sun [made] spring" (p. 51), and here, at the end of his third adventure, he observes the "sudden openness of summer" when "everything seems to hang in the air" (p. 63). The oppressive weather is about to change; the hero directs attention to "an impending storm":

The day comes and goes,
the far vistas of the west
are piles of clouds and
an impending storm. I see
it all now—nothing more.
(p. 65)

THE CONFLICT

Traditionally, the hero of romance struggles with a monster, and the outcome of the battle affects him as well as the people in whose behalf he has fought. Though he need not actually kill his adversary, he must distinguish himself in such a way that he is recognized as a hero worthy of appropriate rewards. In keeping with the conventions of romance, the hero of *Pieces* meets a monster who has "devoured us all" (p. 69). His three attempts to subdue this sea creature are occasions for him to review those ideas about thinking, love, and poetry which have shaped and informed the sequence from the start rather than opportunities for him to display his mastery of logistical tactics. Formally, this summing up amounts to a recapitulation of the themes developed in *Pieces* preliminary to the hero's concluding statements. His final realization that there are no answers to be taken seriously to the questions he has raised in the course of his perilous journey entitles him to his reward, a "delightful" meeting arranged by his "insistence" with "the goddess or woman// become her" (p. 81).

The conflict between the monster and the hero takes place on a beach in Mazatlan. In "Mazatlan: Sea," the opening poem of this section, the beach scene is described both literally and in terms of its metaphysical significance. The hero, characterized here again by his "flat" vision, scans "the sea flat out" and the red sky. The "blobs of dark clouds/ seem closer," he notes, but beyond these signs of a coming storm there is a clear sky. The promise of light after darkness foretells an optimistic resolution of whatever imminent problems threaten to disrupt the beach.

From his vantage point on the beach, the hero, in the midst of oppositions and conflicts, glimpses a possibility which resolves these confusions into a lovely harmony:

> Shimmer of reflected
> sand tones, the flat
> ripples as the water
> moves back—an oscil-
> lation, endlessly in-
> stinct movement—leaves
> a ribbing after itself
> it then returns to.
>   (p. 67)

The slightly rocking rhythm of the lines, together with the sustained interplay of interior rhymes and half-rhymes ("Shimmer," "ripples," "ribbing," and an analogously functional cluster of similar sounds: "sand tones," "moves back" and "then returns"), suggests the peaceful coexistence of ocean and shore, an instinctive relationship seemingly authorized by an eternal design. Only the arbitrary line breaks, most conspicuously "oscil-/ lation" and "in-/ stinct," hint that a now sentimental poet is superimposing an "endlessly" regular pattern on neutral forces. That the hero explored this possibility earlier in *Pieces* but was forced at once to qualify its validity lends support to such a reading.

In the earlier poem "Two" (from "Numbers"), the hero describes Adam and Eve's innocent way of taking the world on their own terms. By its subject, as well as by its tone and vocabulary, this poem prefigures the passage from "Matzatlan: Sea" cited above:

> When they were
> first made, all the
> earth must have
> been their reflected
> bodies, for a moment—
> a flood of seeming
> bent for a moment back
> to the water's glimmering—
> how lovely they came.
>   (pp. 22–23)

This melodic poem is followed abruptly by the hero's acknowledgment that he is mistaken, in this instance because he assumed he genuinely understood someone else's feelings. His tensely put statement begins: "What you wanted/ I felt, or felt I felt" [p. 23]. The contrast between the fleeting moment of naïveté that presumes harmony in the natural world reflects the prized circumstances of lives intertwined, and the painful moment of realization that the possibility of two individuals actually becoming one is in fact a pretentious projection of the desiring self, warns that relationships of any type are complex and ambiguous rather than simple and predictable.

Though the suggestion is thus made that the hero is ascribing more metaphysical significance to the "endlessly in-/ stinct movement" of the waves breaking on the shore than is realistically warranted, the emphasis in "Mazatlan: Sea" is on his feeling that something profound and ultimately valid is about to happen.

Details once associated with his various failures are now presented as optimistic signs of coming success. Against the background of a menacingly dark sky, for instance, a bird flickers dramatically in "light/ sharp." This provocative bird promises action whereas the silent Athena, "braced like a seabird" (p. 9) against the wind, exasperated the hero. The portentous flash of "light/ sharp" offers an ironic comment on the mysterious powers in the hall of blinding light who also refused to help him. Similarly, the two "green hills" the hero observes "make a familiar/ measure" connect back to the naked breasts of the lustful woman who, though "her eyes" tantalizingly suggested "the depth of all one had thought of" (p. 12), laughed at his attempt to understand; but now these hills are linked with the fertility of nature. Perhaps the most promising sign of success is that the hero is no longer trapped in the hot, drab room in hellish Chicago wondering "Would dying be here?" (p. 39). Instead, he feels comfortable and reassured by the thick air and calming sounds of the sea:

> The air is thick
> and wet and
> comfortably encloses
> with the sea's sounds.
> (p. 68)

His earlier hope to find the key to the *"law/ or/ mystery . . . involved"* (p. 33) proved to be a cruel illusion. At this point in *Pieces*, he is given a final chance to unlock the *"mystery"* by crushing the monster "who devoured us all." He prepares himself for this struggle by contemplating his aim and his strategy. He senses that the outcome of the conflict will have something to do with the nourishing of life itself: "Kids walking beach,/ minnow pools—/ who knows which"; his focus will be on literal reality: "Nothing grand—/ The scale is neither/ big nor small" (p. 68). His review of goals and procedures culminates in his renewed commitment to Zukofsky's idea that events must be perceived directly and assessed without recourse to preconceived assumptions: "Want to get the sense of 'I' into Zukofsky's eye—a locus of experience, not a presumption of expected value."

Zukofsky is thus designated as the wise man who oversees the hero's activities, a device customary in the tradition of romance. The hero's wondrous "sentence/ which// began *it was*" (p. 3) owes its inception to Zukofsky; here, as the sentence moves toward completion, the author of *It Was* is called upon to inspire the hero once more. The poetic effect of integrating Zukofsky's name and attitude into this crucial section in *Pieces,* where the hero is on the verge of discovery, focuses attention on the central image of the sequence. His present activity is thereby introduced as a climactic experience that takes into account all that has gone before; the medley of disjunct details are gathered up into the wondrous sentence that was offered at the start as a present. The advice given the hero by other mentors cited earlier in *Pieces* such as Edward Dahlberg's "No knowledge rightly understood can deprive us of the mirth of flowers" (p. 5) and Charles Olson's "We are/ as we find out we are" (p. 56), also shapes his concluding statement. Nonetheless, it is Zukofsky's silent supervision from the start that provides a measure of continuity and a frame of purpose.

The Monster Appears

"Here now—/ begin!" With this emphatic self-addressed command, the hero attests to his readiness. As a prelude to his climactic adventure he becomes aware of two "lovely" creatures who, in accord with the conventions of romance, guard the monster. One is a Gorgon-like "big/ eared almost feral/ toothed woman" (p. 69). Her appearance brings the various elements of the Perseus legend, alluded to earlier, into play again. The other woman has an erotic appeal; her "face a/glow of some other/ experience." So confronted, the hero waits. *"Days/ later,"* a sea monster is sighted:

> An unexamined hump
> at first of no
> interest lifting out
> of the beach at
> last devoured us all.
>
> (p. 69)

The First Day

The hero's immediate strategy is to try to understand the significance of the monster's presence:

> ". . . I ran out of my cabin, both glad and frightened, shouting, 'A noble earthquake! A noble earthquake!' feeling sure I was going to learn something." [John Muir, *The Yosemite*, p. 59.] (p. 70)

As his documented reference to Muir's similarly futile impulse during an earthquake makes plain, he will learn nothing. His intellectual effort to unravel the implications of the disordering literal event ends with his expressed disgust:

> The kick
> of the foot against . . .
>
> (p. 70)

He is left irritated, "looking for the/ recurrence—// waiting."

Unable to explain away the presence of the "unexamined hump" by considering its actions directly, he attempts to recognize its meaning in his "mind's/ patterns." Yet to relive the event in his imagination leads his thoughts away from what actually happened and toward abstract speculation. The consequence of believing experience to "happen" in the "mind's/ patterns" mocks his intention. The first day's battle ends abruptly with the hero's failure. His final comment owes part of its effect to Pound's well-known metaphor linking abstraction to a greased slide:

> Grease
> on the hands—
>
> (p. 71)

The Second Day

Whereas the hero was preoccupied on the first day by the limitations of both determinative and speculative thinking, his nagging concern on the second day has to do with his relationship with his wife. Though he has an obligation to rout the monster who "devoured us all," thereby solving the *"mystery,"* he is distracted by his own feelings of loneliness. Loneliness tempts him to contrive a world of his mind. The possibility of a peaceful *"there"* is played off against his realization that "here is all there is." The conflict is caused by his unhappy marriage:

> How that fact of
> seeing someone you love away
> from you in time will
> disappear in time, too.

> .

> Here is all there is,
> but *there* seems so
> insistently across the way.
>   (p. 71)

Despite his personal problems, he primes himself for the struggle with the sea creature by reawakening his sense of expectation:

> Here I am still,
> waiting for that discovery.
> What morning, what way now,
> will be its token.
>   (p. 72)

He thinks of the vulnerable people on the beach as representative of all people:

> They all walk by
> on the beach
> large, or little,
> crippled, on the face
> of the earth.
>   (p. 72)

Mindful of his responsibility, he welcomes reassurance from the cradling wind:

> The wind holds
> my leg like
>
> a warm hand.
>
> (p. 72)

He has prepared himself to battle the monster and solve the *"mystery."* Yet once again his personal situation intrudes. The sight of his wife sleeping beside him, her body "a quiet, apparent/ containment," sets off a barrage of comments that speak first to his empty feeling of "singleness" and then to his disgust with the "small facts" and " 'breathtaking banalities' " of his life:

> . . . All the world is
> this tension, you or me,
> seen in that mirror,
>
> patent, pathetic, insured.
> I grow bored with lives
> of such orders—my own
> the least if even yours the most.
>
> (p. 73)

On the one hand, he realizes he must come to terms with "this tension" that suffuses his life; on the other hand, he cannot discover a reason why his boring life has a place in an eternally harmonious design, not long before imaged as "endlessly in-/ stinct movement" of the waves breaking on the shore. Or, to put it in terms of the conceptual framework of the sequence, how can he tell the story he alone knows and, at the same time, deliver a message of affirmation that proposes each as a meaningful place in the world?

He is not Perseus nor was he meant to be. He does not see Medusa "in the mirror" as did the hero whose role he once assumed: he sees himself, "patent, pathetic, insured." The woman sleeping beside him is not the fascinating princess Andromeda he has rescued; rather, her life is even more boring than his own. He asks himself "What would you have/ of the princess," and consoles himself with the rationalization that he would have learned nothing new from "the princess" even if he had met her:

> You will ride away
> into the forest, you will
> meet her there
> but you will know her.
>
> (pp. 73–74)

That the hero of *Pieces* dissociates himself from the Perseus
legend suggests he is beginning to feel unequal to the task of
carrying out his assigned mission though he understands it to be his
specific purpose to do so: "My plan is/ these little boxes/ make
sequences . . ." (p. 74). By the time the moment of confrontation
finally occurs, the hero defines himself as a victim; he identifies
with the sea creature now described as "the tense stricken//
animal":

You see the jerked
movement, in the
rigid frame, the
boy—the tense stricken

animal, and behind,
the sea moves and
relaxes. The island sits
in its immovable comfort.

What, in the head, goes wrong—
the circuit suddenly
charged with contraries,
and time only is left.
        (p. 75)

As the "sun drops," signaling the end of the second day, the hero
wonders what went wrong. He thinks that the "contraries" that
overwhelm him are related to his frustrating relationship with his
wife. His wistful tone here belies his acid comments and the
sarcastic posture he once assumed: "I want you. I am still alone,/
but want you with me." The implication is he would be able to find
meaning in the "small facts" of his life, and thus would be able to
fathom the purpose of his story, if this woman, earlier characterized as the lady with the "opaque face," would return his love.
What began as an attempt to rescue "us all" ends with the hero's
realization that his first necessity is to rescue himself. The
swimmers, unaware of his stated ambitions and limiting inade-
quacies, are safe "in the silver/ glitter. The water slurs/ and recurs.
The air is soft" (p. 75).

The Third Day

By the start of the third day ("the heat rises—/ the whole beach/ vacant, sluggish" [p. 76]), the hero has concluded that he is the source of his problems, which he alone must solve. It becomes clear to him by late afternoon that nature will keep her mysterious secrets. "The sea" and "the slight wind move/ with the/ same insistent/ particularity"; "only the/ children" intuitively find comfort in the "harmony" Nature represents (p. 77). His restlessness notwithstanding, he is bound to the world of "small facts," a situation he cannot extricate himself from by virtue of thought:

> How much
> money is
> there now?
>
> Count it
> again. There's
> enough.
>
>   •
>
> What changes.
> Is the weather
> all there is.
>
> • • •
>
> Such strangeness of mind I know
> I cannot find there more
> than what I know.
>
> I am tired of purposes,
> intent that leads itself
> back to its own belief. I want
>
> nothing more of such brilliance
> but what makes the shadows darker
> and that fire grow dimmer.
>   (p. 78)

Love, as he knows it, is not enough to mitigate the dreariness of his "patent, pathetic, insured" life. Neither is thought. Whether or not he can take refuge in his poetic imagination is now the issue. Fully aware that the poem is a made thing, that it is not a substitute for literal experience but rather an agency through which the unbearable " 'breathtaking banalities' " can be made more bearable, the hero turns to words:

> There was no one there.
> Rather I thought I saw her,
> and named her beauty.
>
> For that time we lived
> all in my mind
> with what time gives.
>
> The substance of one
> is not two. No thought
> can ever come to that.
>
> I could fashion another
> were I to lose her.
> Such is thought.
>
> (p. 79)

THE DISCOVERY

The Recognition

The hero has tested the idea that such "piece" has a place in the harmony of the whole against the "small facts," the " 'breathtaking banalities,' " and the "patent, pathetic, insured" nature of his own experience. Though he recognizes the appeal of an affirmative vision, he can find neither a rational nor an empirical justification for it. He will live as best he can. When the anxieties of reality assert themselves, he will sustain himself by fashioning beauty: "There was no one there./ Rather I thought I saw her,/ and named her beauty" (p. 79). It is not that he presents his particular solution in didactic terms. On the contrary, *Pieces* argues that it is presumptuous for the poet to assume the role of a divinely ordained messenger who can solve the *"mystery."* All he can do is bear witness to his own experience because he feels compelled to tell the story he alone knows "the way of." The purpose of his story, if in fact it has one, is not his concern.

Through a poem, he can transform the inconsequential details of "last night's dream" (p. 80) into a wondrous sentence. He dreamed of a man who fell short and landed "spread-eagled on the sidewalk." In the wondrous sentence, this man was the fool who supposed "angels were waiting to uphold him, if it came about that he leaped from the height" (p. 35), and whose foolishness thus represented the dangers inherent in the solipsistic viewpoint. "Later, in another dream," the hero saw himself "hanging on the side" of the cab of a truck, nearly brushed by the turning wheels. In his dream he was charged merely with "bringing beer somewhere." But in his poem he defined himself as Perseus en route to slay Medusa with "wheel eyes for getting there" (p. 59). In still another dream, he simply walked "to some house through the dark." In his poem, however, he was a seeker of knowledge fated to suffer treacherous descents into dark rooms and through dark, winding corridors. Through the poem, then, the hero can transmute boring "small facts" into fantastic possibilities and fuse fragmentary experiences of thinking and feeling into a lasting whole.

The Reward

The entire wondrous "sentence/ which// began *it was*" (p. 3) is a mode, as Zukofsky says, in which "a writer's attempt not to fathom his time amounts but to sounding his mind in it." The conclusion of the sentence offers the hero the specific opportunity to resolve the various problems he has been concerned with in the course of this sounding process, at least to his own satisfaction. From the start, he debated the use of thought. In conclusion, he celebrates the restful state of thoughtlessness. From the start, he worried about getting a wondrous sentence across to an indifferent world. In conclusion, he celebrates silence as the final act of poetry. From the start, he agonized over his tedious relationship with his unresponsive wife. In conclusion, he celebrates "the ease/ and delight" of his "meeting" with "the goddess or woman// become her," a "meeting" initiated and presumably sustained by his "insistence." This sexual experience—"this was the mystery/ I had come to"—commands the foreground:

When he and I

When he and I,
after drinking and
talking, approached
the goddess or woman

become her, and by my
insistence entered
her, and in the ease
and delight of the

meeting I was given that
sight gave me myself,
this was the mystery
I had come to—all

manner of men, a
throng, and bodies of
women, writhing, and
a great though seemingly

silent sound—and when
I left the room to them,
I felt, as though hearing
laughter, my own heart lighten.
                                        (p. 81)

The Symposium Device

Though the now light-headed hero seems satisfied because he has won over "the goddess or woman// become her," the contradiction between the inner power of the shaping imagination and the outer world of "small facts" has not been resolved. A happy throng rises in celebration around the visionary hero who has pierced the mystery and his willing bride; yet if readers cannot identify with the silent, writhing, mindless manner of these men and women, they will be disappointed surely. As if he had anticipated our startled response to the farce of his conclusion contrived in sexual terms, the hero, in the tradition of the romance, turns to his audience:

What do you do,
what do you say,
what do you think,
what do you know.

(p. 81)

The poetic effect of the final stanza is twofold. First, the sequence ends on a congenial note. The hero has told his story; now he asks that another do so. Second, his invitation serves to characterize the story just told as something designed to entertain rather than something didactic, designed to inform. *Pieces* was a present.

Creeley offers us a resolution of the lonely hero's conflicting impulses which is so ridiculous that it is tantamount to no resolution at all. The hero is unable to draw wisdom apropos the human condition from the mythological world ("the goddess") at one extreme, or from the world of "small facts" ("the woman// become her") at the other, not because he is unwilling but because, *Pieces* argues, it cannot be done.

In *Pieces*, seen from this point of view, Creeley explores various ideas associated with existentialism by assuming the posture as well as the burden of Martin Buber's "free man." Like the free man described in *I and Thou*,[10] Creeley's hero has a gift he must give to the world. To use Buber's words, it is the assurance that "there is divine meaning in the life of the world, of man, of human persons, of you and of me." He must make it clear that "the significance of the situation is that it is lived, and nothing but lived, continually, ever anew, without foresight, without forethought, without prescription, in the totality of its antimony." The free man, and similarly the hero of *Pieces*, can fulfill his mission by bearing witness to his own transformation. Once he attempted to understand the paradox of life; now he accepts a brief moment of peace and realizes that he will never acquire "knowledge from it that might lessen or moderate its mysteriousness." Once he celebrated "that by which this world is thought"; now he knows that lived reality is the key and that everything, including instincts, sensations, and fleeting emotions, "must be gathered into the orbit of its mastery." Once he was concerned with the "world of yonder" but now he is concerned with "this world of ours." Once he felt estranged and believed himself "forsaken by the beings to which he spoke the true *Thou*"; now he knows "that full mutuality is not inherent in men's life altogether" but that "it is a grace, for which one must always be ready and which one never gains as an assured possession."

The curve of feeling in *Pieces* parallels Creeley's changing assumptions throughout his poetic career. Thus a useful way to study his poetry as a whole is to trace his gradual acceptance of the existentialist attitude. In many of his early poems collected in *For Love*, Creeley identified with Monsieur Teste's self-protective sensibility encased in the "armour" of his own cerebral image, eager to dispose of seemingly enduring, irresolvable tensions by thinking them through. Then, in the poems of *Words*, he challenged and ultimately rejected the value of this contrived system to help him lead a satisfying, well-ordered life of clarity and purpose. What seemed to bother him most were his frustrating relationships with other people. He realized that his need to feel a sense of belonging was a matter outside the field of analytical scrutiny and rational argument. Creeley turned to the existentialist writers and learned that personal response and involved commitment, however disappointing, could be sources of vitality, of creativity, and, as Buber says, of his own authenticity.

4

"IN LONDON"

"The poem of the mind in the
act of finding what will suffice."

—Wallace Stevens,
"Of Modern Poetry"

THE FORM

The first half of *A Day Book* (1972) is a prose record of Creeley's day-to-day experience. This section, based on family life, gives the volume its apt title. The second half is a sequence of poems inspired by travel and called "In London." As M. L. Rosenthal has pointed out in his critique, the two parts complement each other: "Almost half the book's approximately 165 pages is made up of prose entries in a journal; the rest consists of poetic entries, often parallel or at least reciprocal to the prose."[1] Creeley tends in his writing to explore his preoccupations at the time, regardless of which particular form the writing takes. For instance, his short stories collected in *The Gold Diggers* and his novel *The Island* are, in the main, thematic companion pieces to his poems in *For Love* and the first part of *Words. Listen*, a radio play, and *Presences, A Text for Marisol*, an autobiographical novella, deal with many of the same issues considered in *Pieces* and *A Day Book*. Despite Creeley's feeling that "distinctions between the forms are purely technical,"[2] that his work is "a continuing song, so that no division of its own existence can be thought of as being more or less than its sum,"[3] his poetry can stand free of the rest. The focus in this chapter is on the poetic sequence "In London" itself.

The epigraph for "In London"—"But what to do and/ what to do next?"—is taken from William Carlos Williams's *A Voyage to Pagany*. This allusion is appropriate for several reasons. Both works concern travelers who set out with serious intentions and high expectations. *A Voyage to Pagany* is a subjective account of the year-long European trip Williams made in 1924, a sabbatical from his medical practice in Rutherford he arranged partly in response to Pound's urging: "You'd better come across and broaden your mind."[4] When Dr. Evans, the protagonist, arrives in Pagany (Europe) he is not quite sure what he is looking for but he hopes he will discover values of elemental profundity: "Something may happen" to rearrange his life.

> He wondered what luck he would have on this trip. And always he kept saying: Perhaps this is the time. Something may happen and I shall not return.
> But what to do? and what to do next?[5]

Similarly, the unnamed wanderer in "In London" attaches life-ordering significance to a series of trips through London, St. Martin's in the French West Indies, Belgium, and New England: "I wanted to find something/ worthy of respect."[6] Like Dr. Evans, he hopes "to/ get all the confusions at last/ resolved"; and like Dr. Evans, he learns that his own interests and idiosyncrasies are more to the point than any of the places he visits. Both travelers return home with renewed interest and fresh energy, perhaps because nothing of remarkable importance happens to Dr. Evans to keep him in Pagany and, similarly, because Creeley's protagonist is unable to resolve the confusions. It is not that he is able to solve them at home; rather, it is that "all the confusions" seem to trouble him less in Bolinas than elsewhere.

Both Creeley and Williams subordinate descriptions of topography and manners to their emphasis on the narrator's personal impressions and responses. Dr. Evans's self-directed reflections taken together constitute the real subject of Williams's most lyrical novel. In his introduction to *A Voyage to Pagany*, Harry Levin says this novel "cannot be regarded as a travel book"; instead, he calls it "a spontaneous flow of autobiographical reality."[7] According to Levin, Williams relied heavily on the diary he kept in 1924 "to nudge his memory" which in turn helped him create the illusion of artless spontaneity.[8] Creeley, more daring, offers us his unrevised journal entries in their strict chronological sequence. "In London" is a compilation of loosely connected insights set down on-the-spot: some are related to particular cities and the associations they bring to the speaker's mind but most are self-contained observations of his own nature. These poems, then, are not unified by the poet-traveler's itinerary but by his distinct personality and by his recurrent preoccupation with death, love, and home.

Creeley's decision to present "a spontaneous flow of auto-biographical reality" is the logical consequence of his current attitude toward his poems. An appreciation of "In London" depends to an extent on an appreciation of Creeley's present aesthetic rationale. It is useful, therefore, to outline the changes in Creeley's thinking about the publication, composition, and organization of his poetry through the years with a view toward defining his recently formulated aesthetic reflected in "In London."

From the time Creeley entered the world of letters he was determined "to get his poems out where they ought to be" as quickly as possible.[9] Thus, he established the Divers Press on Mallorca in 1954 to print his own work and work by his friends. For the same reason, he sent individual poems to sympathetic editors in reply to their questions about his current work. He also welcomed the publication of a group of poems in a small pamphlet as soon as the opportunity occurred. To offset the limitations of his free-wheeling publication policy, Creeley selected what he considered his finest poems written during a particular time span for the important Scribner's volume and arranged these poems to complement each other. For instance, he chose the best from among his earliest poems for Part 1 of *For Love* (Scribner's, 1963), subtitled the section "1950–1955," and altered the chronology in several places to achieve a particular curve of feeling. The dozens of poems he wrote between 1950 and 1955 but rejected for the Scribner's volume could still be found in little magazines such as *Origin* and *Black Mountain Review* as well as in five hand-set chapbooks: *Le Fou* (1952), *The Kind of Act Of* (1953), *The Immoral Proposition* (1953), *A Snarling Garland of Xmas Verses* (1954), and *The Whip* (1957).

Creeley's first major statement about his changing attitude toward publication came in July 1967, when he wrote a preface to *The Charm*, a collection of poems written during the fifties but omitted from *For Love*. In this preface, he explains that when he first began writing he was "very didactic and very involved with 'doing it right!' "[10] He therefore debated the merit of each one of his poems and dismissed those he felt were unacceptable.

> . . . whenever there was a chance to publish a small pamphlet or book, my temptation was to cut from it any poem that did not seem to me then and there to make adamant sense as a *poem*, and consequently I tended to ignore a kind of statement in poetry that accumulates its occasion as much by means of its awkwardnesses as by its overt successes.

Creeley goes on in this preface to explain how he came to realize that poetry "that accumulates its occasion . . . by means of its awkwardnesses" should be offered seriously to the general public. He refers to a conversation with Ginsberg during the 1963 Vancouver Poetry Conference that convinced him poetry should reflect "the fact that we are human beings and do live in the variability of that order," including the awkward. Thus Creeley justifies the publication of his early and uncollected poems.

Creeley's enthusiasm for his awkward early poems, first expressed in the 1967 preface ("Selfishly enough, I can often discover myself here in ways I can now enjoy having been—no matter they were 'good' or 'bad' ") determined the final shape of "In London." The sequence is an all-inclusive record of his poetic activity from October 1968 to June 1971. It is not surprising that virtually all of these poems were printed earlier in one of a variety of magazines ranging in character from the ephemeral *Best & Co.* to the established *Partisan Review*, or in slim pamphlets devoted exclusively to his most recent work, *In London* (Bolinas, California: Angel Hair Books, 1970) and *St. Martin's* (Los Angeles: Black Sparrow Press, 1971), to name two of them. What is new is that Creeley persuaded Scribner's to publish all of these two-hundred-odd presumably unrevised poems in the precise sequence in which they were written.

The preface to *The Charm* also makes it plain, however, that more was at stake than Creeley's decision not to offer Scribner's a selected volume. At the same time that he began to consider the merit of his awkward poems by different standards, he began to explore the possibility of spontaneous composition. He thanks Ginsberg, both in the 1967 preface and more explicitly in an interview taped several months later, for reassuring him that an alternative to his previous method of reworking, polishing, and judging his writing did exist, that is, "the possibility of *scribbling*, of writing for the immediacy of the pleasure and without having to pay attention to some final code of significance."[11] Creeley also acknowledges his debt to Robert Duncan, who convinced him that poetry of impulse has an integrity of its own because "there is a place for everything in the poem."[12] Duncan, Creeley says in his preface to *The Charm*, "always insisted, with high intelligence, I think, that poetry is not some ultimate preserve for the most rarified and articulate of human utterances, but has a place for *all* speech and *all* occasions thereof."

One of the first results of Creeley's spontaneous method was "A Piece," a poem written in 1966, which reads "One and/ one, two,/ three," and about which he says:

> When *Words* was published, I was interested to see that one of the poems most irritating to reviewers was "A Piece"—and yet I knew that for me it was central to all possibilities of statement.[13]

"A Piece" was not important because it became a model; there are comparatively few of its nature in *Words, Pieces,* or "In London." Rather, the poem "was central to all possibilities of statement" because it signaled to Creeley that he had gained a freedom in writing which allowed him to write for his own pleasure, "to forget that kind of signification that formal criticism insists on."[14] This newfound sense of freedom enabled him "to include a far more various kind of statement" in his poetry than his pre-1966 habit of writing almost exclusively "in a small focus, in a very intensive kind of address" made possible.[15]

By the time Creeley wrote *Pieces*, he was able to compose a diversity of poetic statements which ranged from the emotionally taut, his trademark, to the frankly trivial. As Denise Levertov has noted in her review of *Pieces*, he was moving away from what she calls "evidences of intelligence," carefully wrought early poems, many "of a ravishing perfection":

> In *Pieces* something different happens—or is *happening*, for it is anything but a static work. Somebody glancing through it who did not know Creeley's earlier books might get an impression of sloppiness and ask, "What's this guy think he's

doing, publishing unfinished drafts?" Someone who knew and
dug his work, its elegance and concision and (most of the
time) its clarity—dug it just for those attributes—might
similarly think *Pieces* weak, self-indulgent, a falling off. But
it's not. Its very sprawl and openness, its notebook quality, its
absence of perfectionism, Creeley letting his hair down, is in
fact a movement of energy in his work, to my ear: not a
breaking down but a breaking open.[16]

The "sprawl," the "openness," and the "notebook quality" Levertov discerns in *Pieces* are equally apparent in "In London." The
chief formal difference between the two sequences has to do with
the organization of material.

Though the structure of *Pieces* is substantially more flexible than
the rigid thesis-antithesis pattern of his early poems collected in
For Love, and more flexible than the loosely associational form of
the long poems in *Words,* the romance convention shapes *Pieces*
overall. With "In London," Creeley ventures into the "FIELD"
Olson defines in "Projective Verse": "From the moment he
ventures into FIELD COMPOSITION—put himself in the
open—he can go by no track other than the one the poem under
hand declares, for itself."[17] "In London" moves seemingly in accord
with the poet's unforeseeable impulses, not in accord with any a
priori plan.

Despite the fact that Creeley has been associated with Olson and
"Projective Verse," it seems that it was Ginsberg who was able to
persuade him that the form of the whole should not be predeter-
mined but should "follow the sequence of perception in the course
of the writing, even if the route became as irrational, intuitive, and
discontinuous as the shape of the mind itself."[18] Ginsberg, identified with a poetry of "undifferentiated consciousness," absorbed
the idea from William Burroughs, who relied on the "cut-up"
method to externalize, dramatically, what "is happening," and
from Jack Kerouac, who wanted prose and poetry to record "an
undistrubed flow from the mind." Kerouac's "The Essentials of
Spontaneous Prose" and Olson's "Projective Verse" have so much
in common that Kerouac could complain convincingly in his *Paris
Review* interview: "I formulated the theory of breath as measure,
in prose and verse, never mind what Olson, Charles Olson says. I
formulated that theory in 1952 at the request of Burroughs and

Ginsberg."[19] The question of who formulated the mid-twentieth-century American version of the theory of spontaneity is not the issue. The central point is that the unusually free notion of juxtaposition that orders the open literary structure of "In London" was probably influenced more by the Kerouac-Ginsberg-Burroughs nexus than by Olson. It may be that Creeley is acknowledging a debt to Burroughs[20] in the following passage from "In London":

> Small dreams of home.
> Small of home dreams.
> Dreams of small home.
> Home small dreams of.

But whether or not Creeley was thinking of Burroughs is not important. The importance here is bound up with the emphasis on spontaneity, the key word linking the theories of the Beat poets and of Olson.

Though Creeley has been called a projectivist poet since the publication of Olson's "Projective Verse" in 1950, "In London" is the first collection of poems that show he has completely assimilated ideas about a poetry of process, ideas associated with projectivism. Too much attention has been paid to Creeley's statement—quoted by Olson in his essay—that "form is never more than an extention of content," a definition of lyric poetry Creeley knowingly borrowed from Valéry.[21] Not enough attention has been paid to the fact that until "In London" Creeley did not allow the form of the whole "to go by no track other than the one the poem under hand declares, for itself." Creeley's actual contribution to "Projective Verse" concerned not the form of the poem but the form of the line. Portions of his letters to Olson in which he responded to Olson's insistence that the poetic voice must be true to the complexities of the human speaking voice—ranging in scope from idiomatic ease to antiidiomatic stammering—became part of the seminal essay:

> And then those letters actually became incorporated finally in that essay on projective verse—in the first section, where he is talking about the significance of the syllable, the sense of breathing, the sense of where the intelligence is operating and the choice of the language where the whole physiology of man is at work in the poem.[22]

Even in his earliest published poems, Creeley was able to make the individual line register his "sense of breathing," though it was often with Olson's help.[23]

Between the time Creeley said "form is never more than an extension of content" and the time he made full use of the idea that content is revealed by form, more than twenty years had passed. In 1971, Creeley explained to Michael André why free form, the theory he spoke about during the late forties, became a workable mode for him at last. Contrary to his previous tendencies, he was able "to trust writing." If he were not completely comfortable with words "by the age of forty or forty-five," he reasoned, it was "obviously too late to learn."[24] Feelings such as these led Creeley to believe that the rhythm of life as it was actually lived, as he recorded it on impulse in his journal, would provide the organizing principle for the sequence. The unpolished, experiential sequence, "In London," reflects his decision to trust to the writing "to locate coherence in the most diverse and random of occaions."[25]

To help induce the effect of untampered-with immediacy the sequence attempts to convey, the pages are unnumbered, and many of the poems untitled. Creeley explains that "there was no need to draw a distinct formal line around each poem as though it were some box containing a formal statement."[26] The poems are separated by dots: "three dots indicate that that was the end of a day's accumulation, and the single dots most usually indicate division in the writing as it's happening, as I was sitting down to do it."[27] This conspicuously casual format—a visual testament to the spontaneity of the whole—thrusts the several motifs which naturally recur thoughout this unrevised travel dairy into the forefront.

The Content

In an attempt to mediate an argument between Creeley and Corman in 1951, Olson wrote to Corman:

> . . . That is, Creeley, is a subtle & beautiful man, worth more than all the rest of us you have published—and then some. Your magazine *Origin* shall be known in the history of writing because you there first published the stories and letters of this

> man. . . . You see, Cid, he is a grave and serious man, & his work of an order that causes him to demand back what he gives: utmost care & openness in discussion of. On top of that, he has, like any of us to whom the thing is already our life stretching down to our death, a sense of responsibility of the act of writing by anyone anywhere . . .[28]

Though Olson felt Creeley's effectiveness as a writer derived in part from his sense of life's wholeness, from his mature understanding as a young man that "the thing is already our life stretching down to our death," Creeley seldom dealt with life as a total experience in his poetry, and he rarely mentioned death. With the exception of a silent elegy for his stepdaughter Leslie which begins "For you there ought/ to be words as something/ at least to say" (*Words*), and several passing references to his father's death, Creeley avoided the subject.

A central issue in "In London," however, is the inevitability of his own death. Milestone events, usually associated with middle age, such as the death of his close friend or the sudden realization that his daughter Kirsten is "a woman now/ entirely," add to his concern with the fact that he is getting old. Minor events, some only related peripherally to aging, gain significance because he views them in the light of his preoccupation. For instance, a slight illness becomes a somber occasion for reflection: "The senses of one's/ life beginning/ to fade." That his "eye seems/ to blur at close print" leads him to philosophize sadly: "Pieces/ fall away dis-/ closing another place." "A sense of time passing surely" frames the whole.

His death, he fears, is almost at hand. Near the beginning of "In London," this all-pervasive theme is introduced in explicit terms and considered at length:

> What is the
> day of the
> year we
> sit in with
> such fear.
>
> WE'LL DIE
> soon enough,
> and be dead—

whence the whole
system
will fade from my head—

"but why the
tort-
ure . . ." as if

another circumstance
were forever
at hand.

      •

Thinking of dying
à la Huxley on
acid so that
the beatific smile his
wife reported
was effect possibly
of the splendor of
all *possible* experience?

Or else, possibly,
the brain cells,
the whole organism,
exploding, im-
ploding, upon
itself, a galaxy
of light, energy,
forever more.

      •

Die. Dead,
come alive.

At first, the gasping poet, seemingly stunned, sounds virtually hysterical; Creeley achieves this breathy effect by breaking the opening lines on the frontal sound and then by beginning the next line with a frontal sound as well. As the speaker continues to reflect on "dying," his voice relaxes as he regains his composure. He might, he reasons, consider death an appreciated release from life.

Instead of mitigating his apprehensiveness, however, the result of his speculation is to redirect his attention toward life itself. He wonders if his life should or could be different, more satisfying, a question Creeley continually asks himself in his poetry. Tortured by his desire to live "all *possible* experience" in the known world, he consoles himself here with the supposition that death is not an end but a continuance. Thus the poet achieves a measure of control over his fears; the series of poems ends on a note of optimistic resolve: "Die. Dead,/ come alive." The poet has recovered his wit: his own mere words are capable of resurrecting the dead. Nonetheless, the serious issues he has raised in this passage about life and death remain unresolved by his cleverness.

What is wanted is a positive attitude toward death at the least or a sure sense of immortality at the most. The poet has neither. As an alternative to the idea that death is a meaningless finality, Creeley envisions a metaphysical state in which the living are at last gathered up into the eternal flux from which they came, a mystical circumstance analogous to the phenomenon of perpetual energy interchange in the galaxy. Of the several poems in this sequence that focus on the implications inherent in this transcendental possibility, the finest is called "Dying."

If, the poem proposes, he can believe that he as an individual is truly part of a "veritable multiplicity!" then he will be on the way toward finding the reassurance he is after. Creeley does not offer the concept of "oneness" as an accepted fact. Rather the poem, which turns on its first word, celebrates the hope:

> Dying
>> If we are to exist,
>> a *we* of an imagination of
>> more than one, a
>>
>> veritable multiplicity!
>> What a day
>> it is—what
>>
>> one of many
>> days and many people,
>> who live here.

You may bring it
in now
to me. That,

one says, is
the multiplicity—
dying.

Creeley strikes the delicate balance between his longing for faith
and his cynically wise understanding which argues against such
faith. Hence, the poem comes to the verge of making a religion out
of imagining a "veritable multiplicity!" but stops short of it just in
time. With mock authority, the poet announces pompously that he
is ready for death— "You may bring it/ in now/ to me"—thereby
depending on irony to register the tenuousness of his philosophical
position. By the end of the poem, he denies personal responsibility
for the sophomoric idea by shifting the pronoun from "we" to "one
says." Yet belief in a "veritable multiplicity!" would have been the
basis of a magnificently fearless solution. For an instant in the
poem, it seemed to exist: "What a day/ it is—." What the poet
would like to have is played off against what he knows he cannot
accept; this emotional juggling accounts for the tension generated
by "Dying."

When Creeley deals with the idea of a "veritable multiplicity!"
as an established rationale, the result is unfortunate. In a long poem
called "People," the eternal, collective life-force is personified as
"myriad people" who "live// now in everything, as everything."
As one of the myriad, he feels connection with the universe. He
is not "isolated" but believes he has "continuous/ place" in
"visions of// order." These comforting notions related to the idea
of "the myriad" were part of his childhood. As a child, he "knew
where they were" and he assumed his sister "possibly . . . was
one,/ or had been one/ before." Though Creeley says near the
close of the poem "Some stories begin, *When I was young*—/ this
also," "People" itself is not a wistful, backward glance to a child's
vision of immortality. Creeley neither develops his hope concerning the myriad as a fragile possibility about to vanish from his adult
mind altogether, nor does he focus on his actual fear of death,
which compels his present speculations. Instead, he presumes the
reality of the myriad throughout the major portion of the poem as
he does in this passage:

I'll never die or else will
be the myriad people all
were always and must be—

in a flower, in a
hand, in some
passing wind.

Though elsewhere in "In London" Creeley lovingly describes his felt affinity with the natural world within a recognizably human context, in this poem his delight in "a flower" or "some/ passing wind" is subordinated to his assumptions about pantheism. With utter seriousness, he speaks about "myriad people" who "live// now in everything, as everything" as a reasonable man would speak in the company of other reasonable men. However, the thought that there are "little people" who live in "a flower," "a stream of smoke," "under rocks," and even in "every insignificant part/ of your body" so that if you "twist" your finger "you'll/ feel the pain of all/ such distortion" and the voices "will// flood your head with/ terror" is surely not a serious notion.

"People" is burdened by a misplaced emphasis.[29] By dwelling at length on his ideas about the "little people," Creeley effectually sabotages the impact of even the finest passages in the poem; yet his fears about death, which, by implication, spawned these fantastic notions, lurk in the background of the poem and lend a shade of melancholy to the whole. The best poems in this sequence that present the recurrent fear-of-death motif are those in which the speaker's determination to control his apprehensiveness is set against his inability to do so completely.

In a poem titled "Moment," for instance, he thinks about what he should do with the time remaining to him. Though his meditation takes place in a graveyard, he strikes a casual posture by assuming a conversational tone and a utilitarian perspective. The only hint we get that he is troubled, that he is on the brink of losing his composure, is relegated to the naggingly provocative phrase "still preys":

Moment

Whether to *use* time, or to *kill* time, either
still preys on my mind.

> One's come now to the graveyard,
> where the bones of the dead are.
>
> All roads *have* come
> here, truly common—
>
> except the body is moved,
> still to some other use.

Another effective way in which Creeley expresses his fears about death is first to indulge his feelings and then to castigate himself angrily for having done so. Despair followed by self-deprecating contempt is one of the characteristic emotional combinations in Creeley's poetry. In the closing stanzas of "Time," his self-pity predictably gives way to his disgust:

> . . . My time,
>
> one thinks,
> is drawing to
> some close. This
>
> feeling comes
> and goes. No
> measure ever serves
>
> enough, enough—
> so "finish it"
> gets done, alone.

Technically, the poet's struggle with his sadness is made evident through the articulation of the lines "some close. This" and "and goes. No" wherein the punctuation forces the reader's voice to dramatize the pull of continuing on despite the poet's impulses to the contrary. At last, the poet refuses to resign himself to his despair. His various self-urgings culminate in an angry, self-mocking outburst. He must, he demands of himself, adopt a more stoical attitude toward death despite his realization that "No/ measure ever serves// enough."

Within the context of poetic association, his flat pronouncement about the inadequacy of every measure is colored by his previously expressed longing to live "all *possible* experience" before he dies despite his understanding that he will never attain such satisfaction. Again and again in this sequence, the restless poet wonders if he is taking from life all that it offers: "why/ shouldn't there be// the possibility of many lives,/ all lived// as one. I don't know" ("Smoke"). The curve of feeling in "Echo" is typical. The poem begins with a premonition "I'm almost/ done," and goes on to convey his vague, amorphorous discontent:

> Was I never here?
> The hour, the day
> I lived some
>
> sense of it?
> All wrong? . . .

He concludes with defiant resolution that borders on resignation: *"Here, here,/* the only form// I've known." Regardless of how the line "No/ measure ever serves// enough" was intended or how it is interpreted, its impact derives from the poet's feeling that his time is running out. In similar fashion, the effect of many poems in this sequence is molded by this underlying omnipresent foreboding.

Perhaps Creeley's most specific statement apropos of his fear of death comes in "Somebody Died":

> Somebody Died
> What shall we know we don't know,
> that we know we know we don't know.
>
> •
>
> The head walks
> down the
> street with
> *an* umbrella.
>
> •
>
> People
> were walking
> by.
>
> They will think of anything
> next, the woman says.

Everything in this fragmented poem bears away from the fact that

someone died. The effect is to rivet attention on it. The poem
begins with a sample of giddy double-talk, moves on to a
description of the present activity that aims self-consciously at
precision ("*an* umbrella"), and, at the close, repeats an overheard
snatch of conversation. By concentrating on the trivial and the
irrelevant, the poem comments on the speaker's refusal to face the
reality of death, a refusal perhaps cultivated in deference to his
inability.

Creeley's preoccupation with death, which gives this sequence
its distinctive character, lends a sense of urgency to his various
attempts to formulate a suitable attitude so that he might die with
a "beatific smile" as Huxley reportedly did. The idea that he will
survive *"forever more"* because he has a place in the eternally alive
"All" appeals to him; but his efforts to explore the implications
inherent in this transcendental reassurance end dismally. A secular
man by his own assessments as well as by familial predisposi-
tion—his grandmother, he says in "The Teachings," sought out a
long lost son but decided never to speak to the "fool" again when
he tried "to teach her/ religion"—he pits his impulse "to love all/
worlds" he lives in, "to/ love everyone alive!" against his fears.
For a while in the sequence it seems as if Creeley might explore
the possibility that love is enough, that a *"voracious"* outpouring of
affection would infuse life with meaning even in the face of death.
At one point he calls himself the "poet of love" and at another he
defines himself as the embodiment of "love" itself, "tracking
through this/ interminable sadness." His is a "slip-shod insistent
sense of affection—," both eager and receptive:

> Love—
> let it
>
> Out,
> open up
>
> Very,
> very *voraciously*—
>
> Everywhere.
> everyone.

However, the nerve-wracking reality of his suffocating relationship with his second wife, Bobbie, argues in practical terms against

his realization of this hope. The press of time aside, Bobbie is the villain of "In London." In literally every one of the many poems in which he refers to her, his impulse to love is checked, distorted, or blocked altogether. We do not get an account of the dynamics of their problematical relationship. Nor do we get a sense of Bobbie's own situation though we gather that her inner resources are severely limited. Such remarks as "GET IT anyway/ you can but first of all/ eat it" and " 'I don't want/ my tits/ particularized,' " at any rate, show a lack of subtlety. In the main, Creeley gives us the speaker's response to his own frustrations. For him, for instance, her presence often conjures up thoughts of the minimal, the meager: "LOVE'S FAINT trace . . ." and "little bits" of love. He associates her with "the stain of love,"[30] thus laying bare his contempt for sex, a contempt perhaps designed to mask his insistent though unfulfilled need for love. Nonetheless, he refuses to confront the distressing reality of his marriage squarely; he refuses to end it. We are expected, presumably, to conclude that he has been victimized by her and to sympathize with his charitable attempts to reconcile their relationship:

> I DON'T HATE you lately,
> nor do I think to
> hate you
>
> lately. Nor then nor now—
> lately—no
> hate—for me,
>
> for you.

Despite the extent to which he has been disappointed in his marriage, he affirms the necessity of their relationship because he must define himself in terms of love. Even in the delicately ambivalent love song called "The Act of Love," which is his most generous expression in the sequence of his confused feelings for Bobbie, his careful tenderness seems to stem more from his painful, insistent longing to love "Everywhere./ everyone" than from his affection for this particular woman, with whom he always remains hesitant and on guard.

The poet's fear of loneliness accounts in part for his ongoing involvement with Bobbie. His uneasiness at the prospect of being

left alone, often an implicit concern barely beneath the surface in
many of his poems, is repeatedly an explicit issue, as just four of
many similar passages make plain:

     In

bed I yearn
for softness, turning
always to you. Don't,

one wants to cry,
desert me! Have I
studied

all such isolation
just to
be alone?
     (from "An Illness")

   •

Why is it an empty house
one moves through, shouting
these names of people there?
     (from "Rain (2)")

   •

    . . . want

you there,
here, *be*
with me.
     (from "Smoke")

   •

what was the way
which brought us here?
To have come to it alone?
     (from "Roads")

The poetic effect of these passages about loneliness is particularly shaped by the all-pervasive death motif. The poet imagines
death to be the ultimate isolation. What he seems to fear most
about death is that he will be alone; what he seems to want above
all is the assurance that he will be included. If, "In London"

proposes, the assumption about metaphysical "oneness" is beyond credibility, than at least its human counterpart—the feeling of camaraderie—is possible. Within Creeley's poetic world, a sense of belonging with valued friends becomes a substitute for the promise of eternity. Intense though fleeting moments of well-being with friends take on a religious aura. Of the several poems in the sequence that present spiritually suggestive idyllic scenes, the finest is "For Benny and Sabina":

> For Benny and Sabina
>
> So lovely, now, the day
> quiets. What one hoped
> for is realized. All
>
> one's life has
> come to this, all
> is here. And it
>
> continues taking place
> for a long time.
> The day recovers
>
> itself, air feels
> a wet, heavy quiet.
> Grey, if one could see the sky.
>
> I felt around myself
> for something. I could
> almost see you in wanting you there.
>
> It's a hard life at times,
> thoughtful, very careful
> of all it seems to find.

Until anxiety intrudes, the hoped-for sense of serenity is realized: the peaceful, quiet afternoon and the pleasure of unquestioned friendship. Throughout "In London," treasured experiences such as this one are accorded the highest value because they reassure the skeptical poet, who at one point defines himself as a "wondering two-footed/ notion of abeyance," that he has "a *place*" in the world ("Persons"). At ease with Mike and Joanne, he "finds/ happiness// delicious . . ." ("Soup"). "For Betsy and Tom" portrays him as "happy, foolish," slightly drunk, and reveling in the self-abandon possible in the company of friends who share his love of peace: she is "charming in// the peace she so manifestly/ carries with her." As these poems in "In London" attest, serenity has replaced analytical thinking—"I used to/ think of the/ reasons as if I// knew them" ("Song")—as the ultimate desideratum in Creeley's scale of priorities.

A cumulative effect is engendered by these isolated moments of uncompromised loveliness. Taken together, ephemeral instances of well-being create an illusion the poet would like to believe; that is, connection does in fact exist between the one and the many, between people and the world in which they live. The prized serene experience, rooted in credibly human situations with mystical overtones, reaches its epitome in a long poem near the close called " 'Bolinas and Me . . .' " in which the several motifs in the sequence are recapitulated and tentatively resolved. The poet and those he loves stand "in the open clearing" surrounded by a "circle of oaks." "The sun going west, a glowing// white yellow through the woods," makes this place seem a "holy place." It is in this "holy place" that the traveler-poet of "In London" comes as close as he will ever come to achieving a "beatific smile."

The poet's fear of death and loneliness, and his hope for love and serenity, come together to inform a single line that functions as a pleading refrain in this sequence: "I want to go home." "Home" refers both to the literal reality and to the metaphysical possibility; thus the statement is frequently appropriate. However, "I want to go home" is repeated so often in "In London" it comes dangerously close to sounding like a whine. Creeley relies heavily on the reader's willingness to respond to this line with complete sympathy, a ready willingness on the reader's part Creeley initiates and shapes by creating a warm relationship between the speaker and reader from the start of the sequence.

In his *Paris Review* interview, Creeley says: "I feel when people read my poems most sympathetically, they are reading *with* me. So communication is mutual feeling with someone, not a didactic process of information."[31] The poet's deliberate attempt to establish and sustain "mutual feeling" with the reader is a motif *per se* in the sequence. The most obvious way in which Creeley tries to elicit and control the reader's accepting viewpoint is to address him openly and often. About one-quarter of the lines in "In London" are either direct or rhetorical questions as in this early passage:

> *Come fly with me—*like,
> *out of your mind* is
> no simile, no mere
> description—what "mere,"
> *mare, mère, mother—*
> "here then," is what you want.
>
> •
>
> Emily—simile.
> What are you
> staring at?
>
> •
>
> I wanted to find something
> worthy of respect—like
> my family, any one one knows.
>
> •
>
> What are you crossing all
> those out for. A silence lasting
> from then on . . .

Congenial and unpretentious—

> I WAS NEVER SO upset
> as when last I met
>
> another idiot walking by
> with much the same preoccupations as I.

—the poet plainly invites the reader's empathy and tries to maintain this rapport throughout "In London." Apart from creating sympathy for the speaker, the dynamics of the speaker-reader relationship generate energy in the sequence. This, and the fact that the speaker is usually involved in intense conversation either with himself or with seemingly dozens of friends, contributes to the feeling that a great deal is happening in these poems. Creeley would probably want the poetic achievement of "In London" to be measured in terms of how much energy the poem "explodes, im/

plodes, upon itself." When Jerome Mazzaro asked him what he looks for in reading other poets, Creeley answered: "Activity. Energy of thought."[32] From the standpoint of the complex of hopes and fears Creeley wrestles with in "In London," "Activity. Energy of thought" is a firm assertion of life though death is near.

The poems of "In London" follow the poet-traveler on his way "home." They show that he makes what he can of his condition with the means available to him. Unable to alter his essentially rational viewpoint, he considers the mixture as he finds it, the loneliness of it, the final tragedy of it, the peace of it. Once home in Bolinas he wonders about "all the confusions" still. But such activity has come to a quiet point, temporarily. The last paragraph of Creeley's recent essay "The Creative" would make a fitting conclusion to "In London," which ends with an essentially similar interplay of settled and unsettled feelings and ideas:

> If I could just create the kind of world I'd really like to live in . . . *I* wouldn't be there. "I" is an experience of creation, which puts up with it no matter. There's a lot to get done. You've been born and that's the first and last ticket. Already he changes his mind, makes the necessary adjustments, picks up his suitcase and getting into his car, drives slowly home. He lives with people whom he has the experience of loving. It's late. But they'll be there. He relaxes. He has an active mind.[33]

APPENDIX

The first part of what follows is a portion of a conversation I taped with Creeley at his home in Placitas, New Mexico, in May 1975. Although we talked for five or six hours, the only poems we discussed were"Return," his first, and "Helas," one of his first.

On the second tape, which Creeley recorded in August 1975 and called "Talking on Your Notes," he responds to the dozens of questions I meant to ask him in Placitas. He sets his remembered intention or present feeling about writing individual poems against my understanding in reading them.

As I now look over my transcriptions, I am sadly aware that they merely give the reader a slight sense of Creeley's remarkable generosity and quick humor. Let it suffice to say: I am indebted to his good nature.

AT PLACITAS

Edelberg: In "Return," what accounts for the distance between you and "such people"? The war experience? The nature of "such people"?

Creeley: I'd just come back from being in the American Field Service in Burma. I remember my family, then my mother, my sister, and nephew, were all living in Cambridge, so I got off at the North Station and took the subway into Harvard Square. It seems to me it was on Thanksgiving Day that I came home, and I can remember feeling an awfully confused sense. I dearly wanted to see my family again, but to suddenly get out into a classic New England holiday, to step out into that reality with all this war circumstance still much in my head—I stopped in a bar to regroup and people were in characteristic Thanksgiving spirit. Being in uniform, someone bought me a drink. It was the sense of that street and feeling very displaced in relation to it, to the people having this

158

kind of apparently quiet, centered situation of existence, and I felt my head was blown from the war, the insistent, endless chaos, the absolute dislocation it created. So that to suddenly find yourself in a tidy New England scene—I didn't really know at that point whether I wanted to be one of those people or not but I felt that these people with apparent security in their situations, having designated homes, designated doors—there's the impulse of wanting to go through the door and be one of those people but the tacit feeling of the poem to me has to do with waiting, waiting for what will direct you to some subsequent or opening activity.

One of the sad dilemmas of that time was that the content of the war experience was in no way locatable among the people of my life. I remember not long after going over to see if I could relocate an old girlfriend at Radcliffe in one of the dorms. I came in in this battle dress and I'm given a charming flash response from these young ladies. I'm wearing a black patch at that time and I looked kind of dramatic. Well, again, it was useless to me. I really wanted something to locate me. I've been through this extraordinary chaotic time. It isn't that I felt I was owed anything but my college background up to that point had already been dislocating. My relation with my family was warm and emotionally good but it was that characteristic dilemma of their inability—not because they didn't want to understand what it was that I wanted to do or what I thought I had as a possibility or what I really had in mind to accomplish. To add to the chaos of being a college student at that time was this whole war scene which you couldn't report to people. I didn't feel smug—like, "you people don't know what I went through." I didn't feel any drama or heroism, but I felt I can't get these two realities to be in the same world and, even more to the point, I can't find my own situation as relates to either one of them.

I did literally locate this girl who was as dislocated as I was. Really I all but—no, I don't think I forced her to marry me. I think we had the mutual need for somebody to locate so we grabbed on to each other. I think I really did insist upon marriage just to be real, to take up a real role as I assumed it to be.

I did feel extraordinary isolation. The vocabulary in those days was so goddamn insistent upon evidence. This was the heyday of interest in Kafka, for example, or in the Existentialists. Those were the writers that were greeted with real respect and intensity. Or we were reading Dostoevski. All of our favorite authors were heavily into situations of isolation with the possible exception of D. H. Lawrence whose senses of alienation are more interesting to me, finally. Lawrence can obviously qualify the alienation of human experience from the natural event, but he doesn't use it as an intellectual center as, say, Sartre seems to. He doesn't use it as a point of vantage, but he uses it as a point of, almost despair, as a dilemma of consciousness, of being human. Speaking for myself, the authors that really got to me in that time of my life were the great egocentrics like Donne, for example.

What I'm trying to say is that we prided ourselves on liking everything that seemed to argue the arbitrary insistent division of person from any collective. We felt a confidence in that.

Edelberg: It seems to me the social reality described in "Return" is one of threatening rigidity. Or, to put it another way, this is simply not your world.

Creeley: No, it never was. That was always a dilemma because it was truly the world of my sister and my mother. The nexus of my family pattern as a kid was my mother, and my sister, and myself. In that pattern, I know that I felt jealous at times. I would go to bed and hear the women, as I would feel, talking in the kitchen. I was the youngest. My mother was then working as a nurse in Melrose. My sister's marriage had broken up sadly. In any case, she now was staying with my mother. This meant that my mother, sister, and small nephew were the family constitution, so to speak. I felt real love in relation to all, but I felt as though my scene was very disjunct to theirs.

Edelberg: Is the purpose of using alliteration to point up a parallel between New England and Anglo-Saxon rigidities?

Creeley: I don't know how much can be thought of as a conscious intention and how much is effectually a so-called personal style of feeling or saying things. I remember feeling that what I then had to say or write was awfully frail and I was trying, I guess, to give it more solidity by compaction of sounds.

Edelberg: Where does the title word "Helas" come from?

Creeley: I wrote that poem, it seems to me, while living in France, and I must have been attracted to the French word for "alas." I don't even know if I got it right.

Edelberg: Is the phrase "as an axe-edge takes to a stone" an allusion to Olson?

Creeley: Actually, it's from New Hampshire.

Edelberg: Then there's no allusion in your poem to Olson's "La Torre?"

Creeley: What's the name of that poem?

Edelberg: "La Torre," 1951.

Creeley: The first poems of his that I saw were 1948, so that I must have been picking up on—the thing is that I was using Olson's stance, but I don't think—no, I don't think that image literally comes from him. I think the term of address comes from him. Well, go on.

Edelberg: As I understand it, in "Helas" you say that you admire Pound, Olson, and Williams, but at the same time, you satirize these poets' idiosyncracies. Finally, you get tangled in the coils of your own dilemma.

Creeley: Yeah, I suppose. I think Pound is the one who really occurs to me. But I still would feel that the axe—I could be using Olson's—go on.

Edelberg: Why are you reworking Williams's "The Wind Increases," stanza by stanza?

Creeley: I was doing it intuititvely. I knew that poem.

Edelberg: "Helas" makes sense to me as an ironic comment.

Creeley: What can one do, so to speak, where the irony is the unintentional instrument?

Edelberg: If the irony is unintentional, why are the references first to Olson, deliberate or no, and then to Williams, an allusion which must surely be deliberate because it is sustained, both in parentheses?

Creeley: This is a trick or at least a device I'd picked up from Olson—its apparent use was that it seemed to me you could hold two things in mind.

Edelberg: Williams is dismissed. The lines which precede your quotation from "The Wind Increases" connect with the lines which come after it—as if you never heard Williams at all.

Creeley: Yeah, well, I'm sorry. I've been so afraid of irony all of my life. I remember a long time ago I didn't feel comfortable with well—I was very impressed by Pound's authority in the language; that is, the sources of his language. But I knew that, personally, his solutions weren't mine. And from living in New Hampshire I knew that there were real, physical, literal events that were crucial beyond estimation.

Edelberg: Is "Helas" not a parody of Olson's ideal man on the instant, figuring it out, going around in circles?

Creeley: Unintentional, but nonetheless true.

Edelberg: Do you think I've overread this poem?

Creeley: No, I don't think so at all, because the point is that there's, as I think of it now, an obvious testing of the kinds of solution that these various people had. They were didactic. Their solutions were particularly theirs. I've had that with Williams this last year. In this seminar in Buffalo we were reading *Paterson,* when I suddenly felt an inexplicable, almost an anger, at the poem. The interest of the writing was very clear to me—that had stayed put—but the emotional and experiential state he was in was just getting really sticky to me.

Edelberg: You've used Williams's poems often. What are you responding to in his poems about love?

Creeley: I used Williams sadly, unintentionally, as a reassurance that my attitudes in relation to women were not predicated, but that they found company in Williams, and they surely did in many ways. Williams's tacit hostility to women at times is really heavy and I became more and more aware of it as I got older, particularly so in this last year where the reading at times would almost become literally offensive to me. I felt he must know, as a sophisticated and intelligent man, how this constant laying on of this singularized group woman, how complacent that is.

I remember reading *Paterson* as a younger man and feeling a complacent superiority and distaste for this whining, paranoid, and sad woman who's used in *Paterson.* I felt very complacently critical of her as some distraction to the great man and I thought, "Well, isn't it generous of him to include her as part of the record."

This semester I want to center on two books of his which are endlessly expansive—the materials collected in *Imaginations* and the *Collected Earlier Poems*. I think they're incredible periods in his own writing—those two stretches—and really try to locate what the emotional, so-called experiential feeling seemingly is.

Edelberg: Why did you bring Williams into "Helas" and then dismiss him?

Creeley: He was my master in one sense. I had to. He one time wrote me a lovely letter. I'd sent him a poem. I don't even remember what poem it was. He wrote this extraordinary warm enthusiastic first paragraph, incredible really. The whole thing really lands me on my back. It's like an incredibly generous response to a younger poet. Of course, we both know that only happens rarely; nobody has the decision of it. It wasn't that he was being niggardly. In one sense, I quite agree with him now. It is then that kind of ability you can have a possibility of, but don't have a decision of. There's something dear in that letter. I suddenly realized I really got to him as another writer. Yeah, I was competitive. I really wanted to do the best. Duncan in a letter to Olson, that's included in the issue of *Maps* that's given over to Duncan's work, makes a kind of lovely time line pointing out to Olson who would share a particular world view, who would be the olders of, who would be the youngers of. He points out that I'm the youngest to be included in this particular nexus of writers, people, friends, the youngest to be included in the attitude toward the world that is, say, Charles's, Duncan's, Denise's, who would have experienced the depression in a real way. One time Olson said to me in a conversation, "You, me, Duncan, and Ginsberg constitute the four legs of the table." Charles always insisted on an antagonism toward Ginsberg, but he was fascinated by Ginsberg as a public event, jealous of him.

Edelberg: Olson called Valéry a "stuffed bird." Why did you feel drawn to the Monsieur Teste posture?

Creeley: I was fascinated by the Monsieur Teste stance. It was the singular voice. That's an awkward phrase, but I suppose in that rhetoric I was trying to devise a way to state senses with relation to Olson. Charles and I were writing to one another, practicing, at least I was, and I didn't first recognize that he was markedly older than I was. I didn't at first realize that he had established a very real person as a writer. I remember when that occurred. I do remember that vividly. I said to some friend, "Oh, I talked to Olson," and he said, "You must mean the Charles Olson who wrote *Call Me Ishmael."* I said, "I don't think it could be the same man. As far as I know this man is trying to get poems published in much the same sense I am. I don't think it could be the same person." I wrote to him and mentioned it as something kind of funny. Then he sent me a copy of the book, and I read it at one sitting with pleasure indeed. It was a book that hit me like Lawrence—extraordinary impact. I thought, "He's great. He is really great." Then I felt the extraordinary wash of resentment and anger. I felt I'm so far behind in the accomplishment. Remember, I'm this kid from New Hampshire with a wife who was becoming increasingly despondent with what seemed my preoccupation to be a writer. It did seem like we would trail on forever, you know, trying to find some convenience that would let me write. As a matter of fact, years after our divorce, when we got back together, she was amazed to find that I was still writing because it was her sense of the situation that I must have long since given up that futile task.

I was fascinated to know if there was a way of being in a world that would let you participate without committing yourself. I thought you had to stake yourself truly on what you proposed to do. But Monsieur Teste was permitted to have all the cunningness. I remember reading recently Wyndham Lewis, where he is talking of being in the crowd. It's a stance very like Monsieur Teste's where he says every time he'd go out in the street, he would practice meeting with the crowd and describe situations as would a dispassionate observer.

TALKING ON YOUR NOTES

Edelberg: Was "Helas" a private poet's poem in the sense that "La Torre" was known to very few people in 1951?

Creeley: We talked about "Helas" in Placitas. I was fascinated. That reading you gave it really stuck in my mind, so I certainly am not thus arguing with the sense you may have. Was "Helas" a private poem? Yeah, I'm damn sure few people saw "La Torre."

"Helas" has always been interesting to me simply that it is one of the primary poems, possibly the first, that Olson effectually demonstrates an alternative pattern of lining. In a letter wherein he is responding to it, he simply shows me how otherwise it might be lined so that it follows more literally the physical impulse of the statement. I was using then an intellectual logic, or logic based on the intellective movement rather than the physical movement or the emotion or the physical sound. I know that my letter to him survives, and I think that his letter to me does too.

Edelberg: In the dramatic core of "The Innocence"—"It is a mist/ now tangent to another/ quiet"—the poet as I read it is imaged as the "quiet" who pierces the "mist" by pretending "innocence," and is thus able to make fine distinctions.

Creeley: The first or primary mist is the physical, literal, natural mist. The other "mist" is I suppose what one might call a metaphysical "mist." It is the apprehension of a "mist" which is being felt as a distant, faint, but imminent "mist" that is in some ways more difficult, more threatening, but not literally so. One doesn't know as yet what it implies or what is thus its possibility or instance or fact. "It is a mist/ now tangent to another/ quiet." I feel a threat in there but at this point I don't quite know why. I almost think of that sense at edges of sea when things go into that fine, fading fog. It's that kind of circumstance. But, in any case, it is not the poet, and he is certainly not pretending innocence. He is feeling literally innocent, ingenuous.

Edelberg: As I read "An Act of Pity," the speaker's determination to assess the frustrating situation calmly and fairly "masks" his inability to deal with his emotions directly. That is, the self-effacing judgment "because/ I have nothing for you, and am wrong" is a contrived prelude to an angry accusation, is it not?

Creeley: I remember that was written in Mallorca. I think probably the one character in literature that's ever really seemed to me a possibly frightening identification of myself was Uriah Heep. I fear hypocrisy, emotional hypocrisy; that is, I feel a great distaste for it, and I hate its location in terms of my own sense of myself. "An Act of Pity" has an awfully poor-mouthing quality to it. I like its movement, but when you hear said, "Because/ I have nothing for you and am wrong," it's that self-effacing judgment again, and that gets really boring.

Edelberg: What is the relationship between the speaker's account in "The Riddle" and Madame Teste's account? Does the unspecified "particular" in this poem have a literal counterpart?

Creeley: I have no consciousness of that kind of a relationship; that is, of having relations with Madame Teste. My wife then was literally pregnant or, more accurately, had been, and I was struck indeed by the fact that no anticipation of what's to happen ever in any way is comparable to the literal event. I thought, too, of the irony wherewith people have children almost as a possessional right and how curiously, ironically displacing that whole imagination of the event is. I was thinking obviously of it from the point of view of the husband, who frequently—or at least I certainly did then—feels the sense of being apart from the center of reality, left out of it.

Edelberg: What accounts for the speaker's patronizing attitude in "The Business?"

Creeley: "The Business" is an ironic characterization of a love imagined as a transactionary gain. Again I was thinking of certainly then-frequent senses of exchange humanly—that kind of attitude toward marriage as being a bargain. And so the poem has that ironic tone in it.

Edelberg: The last lines of "The Flower" testify to the almost beaten speaker's stamina . . .

Creeley: The flower is elegantly small and wisely faint. I think it is a very coy piece of writing finally, and it is not one of my favorite poems by any means. I'd stand by it, having committed it so to speak. It's not an attitude of myself that I much enjoy. I question that the last lines testify to the poet's stamina. They have to do with a coy sense of victory, I suppose.

Edelberg: "The Letter," "The Place," and "The Hill" turn on various definitions of "form," a key word in *For Love,* Part 2. I'm thinking particularly of the idea that the "form" is the "grotes-/querie," as you say in "The Place."

Creeley: This poem is very close to me. It relates to a place outside of Juárez, an old kind of deserted cafe that had a little outside raggedy garden. Bobbie and I would at times go down to Juárez for the weekend, and this was one of our favorite places, so the poem has to do with a sense of what does memory actually state. Hopefully, there is something more substantial and more interesting than nostalgia in it. What is the "form" is the "grotes-/querie" in that it's an insistence, intellectually argued, that the event per se defines the significant form.

Edelberg: I think the "Ballad of the Despairing Husband" is a parody on the "love songs and petitions" associated with the "cult of amor." That is, where would you find a "coamantis" who would sit still for the last stanzas?

Creeley: "Ballad of the Despairing Husband" has to do with echoes of the translations Paul Blackburn was then doing. This would be in the early fifties, and this poem, I remember, was written at Black Mountain. My first wife, Ann, and I were really at a sad distance. She was in Mallorca. We'd really determined to separate. I suppose I was sentimentally hoping that possibly it wouldn't happen, but I was really getting tired of my own despair. "Where would you find a coamantis who would sit still for the last stanzas?" I was hoping that those were the only things that would make her sit still; that is, I hoped that she still had some virtues of a sense of humor. At that point, hopefully, it turns into fun. And the last lines of the poem are obviously whiningly sincere.

Edelberg: What do you find interesting in Campion's lyrics? The organizational format of the epigram? The music of the plain style?

Creeley: I chose Campion's poem because it had to do with a sense of definition of where I felt myself to be: "Follow thy faire sunne, unhappie shaddowe:/ Though thou be blacke as night,/ And she made all of light,/ Yet follow thy faire sunne, unhappie shadowe." It's that sense of a very complacently self-demeaning reality, not in Campion's language, but again it's a courtly, pre-Elizabethan trip to that point where to me it's a deliberately chosen mask. It's a homage to these writers truly, first to Blackburn's translations, and then to Campion.

I'll tell you what interested me about Campion. Here are some statements Walter Davis makes in his "Introduction" [*The Works of Thomas Campion* (New York: Doubleday & Co., 1967)]:

> That no edition of Thomas Campion has appeared in the nearly sixty years since Percival Vivian's indicates the neces-sity for the reexamination to which the present edition is

dedicated. . . . A major cause for the decline of Campion's reputation over these sixty years was T. S. Eliot's domination of the literary scene in the 1920's and after, with the resultant elevation of John Donne and the "metaphysical" poets to major status as the really important poets of the English Renaissance, and of metaphysical wit and the complex image as the major evidences of literary worth. Eliot's reevaluations soon hardened into dogma: under the shadow of Donne, even Milton's reputation paled, and lesser poets such as Jonson, Campion, and Herrick, who, like Milton, subordinated image to argument, found little or no room in the literary establishment at all. [pp. xiii–xiv]

A little later he is saying, ". . . new British poets such as Donald Davie and Philip Larkin have been more interested in 'purity of diction' and energetic syntax than in image; and we have seen an important American poet like Robert Lowell move from a packed imagistic poetry to a relaxed and plainer epistolary style" [p. xiv.]. That's to the point.

A little later he is saying, "That Campion is the primary poet of the auditory imagination is due to his combining the roles of poet and composer. . . . The concept of the lyric as epigram . . . [p. xxiii].

Now I had none of this as a very conscious attitude toward him, but it is clear to me, almost thirty years later now, that that's what was attractive to me. Even though I really probably only knew three or four poems of his, they stuck extraordinary in mind. I still quote them.

Edelberg: Hugh Kenner cites "Oh No" in an article in the *National Review* and goes on to say, "*A Form of Women* is very likely one of the books for which everyone will be combing secondhand lists in ten years." What most interests me about "Oh No" is its tone. How would you describe it?

Creeley: "Oh No" is again self-parody, a parody on the situation of feeling that I was having. Irony. These are wry. As Joel Oppenheimer said, that would qualify me to be a Jew. He really liked that poem. It's that kind of humor.

Edelberg: Would you prefer to exchange "words" for "wood" and "voice" for "hands" and thereby achieve a tactile, physical material for your art? It seems to me that in "The Figures" you consider this impulse.

Creeley: Yeah, I'd love to have words to be as substantial as the material of wood. I think they are, frankly—and "voice," as you say, for "hands". I love to feel that substantiality in the activity. I like the movement of this poem very much. The deliberate consciousness of its attitude gets a little heavy for me now, but I love the pace of the poem. I think its gets to "quiets," so to speak, which are very attractive to me.

Edelberg: What has the authority of silence and the power of stillness to do with a "proper form"? Mallarmé's Hérodiade says, "I am indeed alone, O charm and curse!" Is this the line that inspired "After Mallarmé"?

Creeley: I was later told that the poet I was actually translating was not Mallarmé but Jouet. I'd met Phillip Guston in the middle fifties when teaching at Black Mountain. He was a very generous and bright and warmhearted man who had an extraordinary range of information in reading and writing. I'd gone up to his studio to see work he was to have in his first show, and he quoted that poem to me. When I got back to where I was staying I did some rough notes remembering his translation of it and gave him that poem. So you'd have to ask the actual writer—who ain't me—"Why is this the proper form?" I think all language moves to be silent in a curious way. It moves to that, not resolution in the sense that there we settle the argument, but it moves to that sense of fulfillment that lets it pass into silence.

Edelberg: The poet in "The Plan," both victim and torturer, agonizes over the possibility that "truth" ("something that would make it all less silly") may be "trapped" by the mind after all. Isn't this the "most sought, most unsought moment" as in "The Riddle"?

Creeley: Yeah. I was trying to think what can surprise one out of the extraordinarily awkward patterns that one can think up to make reality accessible and malleable. Kids, sentimentally or not, are proposed as having some consciousness not so limited, but adults disastrously do seem to find themselves locked into game plans that can be extremely destructive to their lives. One can plot literal events, but to rob them of their own facts is diminishing because it does not permit an experientially true sense of existence.

The poem is trying to qualify and put down that kind of plotted reality.

Edelberg: In "The First Time," the speaker generously, but decisively, attempts to relegate past mistakes to the past, and I question his sincerity. Is he speaking from a sense of conviction or from a sense of necessity?

Creeley: There are several obvious emotional reasons for wanting to relegate past mistakes to the past—a first marriage that had really been destructive. I feel conviction. I mean no one was—there was literally nothing in the situation that was asking it of me, except possibly my own feelings, of course. But insofar as that was true, I felt, without question, sincere in that poem. In fact, poems permitted me that sincerity at times, in ways that personal statement otherwise wouldn't.

Edelberg: There is a sense of sequence about the poems in *For Love.* Have you ever considered grouping poems by theme and thereby strengthening the narrative line?

Creeley: No, I didn't. I have never considered grouping poems by theme, because theme is like the hidden thread in what I'm writing, rather than the conscious focus. My interest in the writing is the technical pattern. What else is manifest seems to be what's there to be said, at least that's the one substantial conscious thread that I've paid attention to. Especially in earlier poems, the ups and downs of thinking and feeling would be really awkward to attempt to follow as theme. In fact, it would be very, very painful to try. The first situation where I really consciously focused on these would be sequences such as "Numbers" and, more recently, when I have been working in prose where I have a thing in mind that I center upon to use the various experience of to get at diverse material then active.

Edelberg: In the Introduction to *Whitman Selected by Robert Creeley* you describe Whitman's pattern of organization in *Leaves of Grass* as "agglomerative." *Words,* it seems to me, is an "agglomerative" text; that is, most of the poems carry the three major themes along simultaneously.

Creeley: What you are saying makes sense to me but I don't think, though, it has anything to do with intention. I've been recently trying to get together a *Selected Poems.* I first thought to include substantial sections; that is, whole books like *For Love*. It began to be so close to a *Collected Poems*, I gave the job over to a generous friend, Bob Grenier, who's done a really handsome job of it. So anyhow, I have been able to think of these patterns of collections as being instances, not only of time and place, but of ways in which I was trying to think through or get hold of various circumstances that were variously problematic. *Words* is a crucial book for me. It begins toward the end to really depend on what you call "agglomerative" structure, which has become increasingly useful to me.

John Chamberlain is a friend, an old friend indeed, an extraordinary sculpturer. His comment on the book was that it was full of measuring. It's true. A lot of poems in the book are involved in ways in which reality can be, not assessed as by putting a value upon it, but ways in which it can be located by measure, like finding the coordinates necessary to the recognition of where it's at.

Edelberg: Several poems in *Words* deal with what traditionalists call love—getting it, losing it, trying to make peace with its power. Some of these poems, such as "Hello," "A Sight," and "The Hole," have the distinction of being the most physically aggressive in a generally congenial, however intense, corpus.

Creeley: I really respond particularly to what you're saying here. There's a lovely series of three prints that R. B. Kitaj did with my handwritten text of "The Sight." I really can't describe it to you—you'll have to see it—but the final image is effectually a lovely ghost figure, a bad ghost with a very straight line acting as a cord around its neck, this crazy shaking motion surrounding it, little lines of visible activity thus caught fixed by the string. It was emotionally a very hard time in our lives—a daughter's death unexpectedly in a sudden accident. I came to Buffalo in 1966, and things became very much more simple, financially. We did move out of the very pinchness that we had as a family; that is, having no money, etc. But also it was a time of much restlessness for us and confusion at times in our relationship. The book certainly has that tone. This book is much concerned with emptiness. It has all the sexual overtones. The only dilemma I now find in that would be that the sexual overtones might push aside all the other nature of emptiness that's there.

Edelberg: As I understand it, the hero of *Pieces* is, as a poet, compelled to deliver a visionary message of reassurance: each "small fact" of literal experience has its "place" in the "endlessly in-/ stinct movement" of the whole. At the same time, the hero is caught up in his personal cynicisms, interests, and frustrations. The formal key to the sequence is bound up with the "agglomerative pattern," a version of Zukofsky's zig-zag "story of our time." The contextual key to *Pieces* has to do with Zukofsky's concluding line to *It Was:* "You were good to me," a feeling which is designated in your sequence as "Happy Love." That is, the key to the transcendental vision in *Pieces* is "Happy love."

Creeley: I really like what you have to say of *Pieces,* particularly "the key to the transcendental vision is 'Happy love.' " Zukofsky's "You were good to me"—I'll never forget that. I'd just been reading Zukofsky's *A-22,* which I think is an extraordinary sequence, and the reality there insisted upon is the one absolutely compatible with my own hope. *Pieces* is again an "agglomerative" text, a zig-zag story of our time.

Edelberg: In *The Finger,* "In London" is the title poem of a sequence that ends with "The Song Of." In *A Day Book,* "In London" is the title poem that seems to include all the material that follows it.

Creeley: My English publishers are understandably intent not to have their publications be simply facsimiles or simply be repetitions of the American publications. They like a little overlap, something that distinguishes their publication. These poems can be read variously as a sequence of single poems or as a cluster of writing. Just be careful that you don't make some proposal that says they have an attitude on the part of the writer that is developing consciously, e.g., like *Four Quartets.* There is no such proposal of that kind of unity here at all. It's an experiential unity, not an intellectual one, if any.

FOREWORD

1. Robert Creeley, *Contexts of Poetry: Interviews 1961–1971*, ed. Donald Allen (Bolinas: Four Seasons Foundation, 1973), p. 18.

INTRODUCTION

1. Unpublished autobiographical note of June 26, 1966, at Washington University. As cited by Mary Novik, "Robert Creeley: A Writing Biography and Inventory" (Ph.D. diss., Univerity of British Columbia, 1966), p. 5.

2. Creeley, *Contexts*, pp. 148–49.

3. Ibid., p. 148.

4. Ibid., p. 147.

5. Ibid., p. 148.

6. Ibid., p. 146.

7. Creeley often refers to himself in his poetry as one-eyed, but he rarely writes about his handicap in extended terms. This passage from *Presences, A Text for Marisol*, is one such unusual instance. His account of a bitter childhood episode belies the conspicuously calm posture he assumed in the autobiographical note written years earlier. This is in keeping with Creeley's increasing ability to discuss painful experiences in a more candid fashion as his recent poems attest:

> . . . I had a glass eye that would with my rubbing at it as the school day got tedious occasionally fall out and roll across the floor under the desks. Always some pleasantly intrigued and brave kid would pick it up, ask permission to leave his seat, and bring it back to me. I would rub it with my handkerchief, an instance of which I still compulsively keep with me, though the eye itself is long gone, and put it back in. At recess kids I wasn't friendly with would tease me by asking, did I take it out with a spoon, and then plead to see it. Was it round and so forth. One so maddened me I remember jumping him and finally pounding his head against the metal supports for the swings until friends of us pulled me off. (*Earth Geography*, booklet no. 3 [Cape Elizabeth, Maine: Io Publications, 1972], p. 203)

8. Autobiographical note as cited by Novik, "Robert Creeley," p. 6.

9. Creeley, *Contexts*, p. 149.

10. Autobiographical note as cited by Novik, "Robert Creeley," p. 6.

11. Ibid.

12. Creeley, *Contexts*, p. 139.

13. Ibid., p. 48.

14. Robert Creeley, *The Charm* (San Francisco: Four Seasons Foundation, 1969), p. 3. Most of the poems in *The Charm* were written during the fifties but not selected for *For Love: Poems 1950–1960*, Creeley's first important publication. Although from time to time I shall refer to poems in *The Charm*, I do not include this volume in my study because the poems collected here do not indicate the way in which Creeley's poetic voice will develop. Furthermore, the poems themselves have little merit. In his preface to *The Charm*, Creeley

apologizes in advance and warns the reader will find in the volume the kind of poem "that accumulates its occasion as much by means of its awkwardnesses as by its overt successes." (Other quotations from this volume will be cited by page in the text.)

15. Novik, "Robert Creeley," p. 9.

16. Creeley, *Contexts*, p. 47.

17. Ibid., p. 50.

18. As cited in Robert Creeley, *A Quick Graph* (San Francisco: Four Seasons Foundation, 1970), p. 4. Frederick Eckman, the editor of *Golden Goose*, pointed out in his review of *All That Is Lovely in Men* that two poems, "Broken Back Blues" and "Stomping with Catullus," are "free-swinging variations" influenced directly by jazz.

19. "Talking On Your Notes." In September 1975 Creeley made a tape for me on which he sets his remembered intention or present feeling about a poem against my understanding of it. The substance of our conversation appears in the Appendix.

20. Creeley, *Contexts*, p. 140.

21. There are 354 letters from Creeley to Corman at Indiana University. The first one is dated 14 December 1949. (Creeley says the magazine "happily" gave him "business" to write to Pound and Williams about.)

22. Letter at the University of Connecticut as cited in *Athanor* 4 (1973):59.

23. The letter, dated 21 April 1950, was published in *Maps*, no. 4 (1971), p. 8. I have tried to reproduce Olson's typography and where this was impossible I have tried to approximate it. Ferrini sent Olson's "Lost Abroad" and "The Laughing Ones" to Creeley.

24. Hugh Kenner, *The Pound Era* (Berkeley: University of California Press, 1971), p. 506.

25. Michael Reck, *Ezra Pound: A Close Up* (New York: McGraw-Hill, 1971), p. 107. For detailed study see Charles Olson, *Charles Olson and Ezra Pound: An Encounter at St. Elizabeth's*, ed. Catherine Seelye (New York: Grossman Publishers, 1975). Through Olson's agency, Pound learned about the workings of the Washington bureaucracy. Through Pound's agency, Olson's study of Melville, *Call Me Ishmael*, was published, as was his essay, "Projective Verse."

26. Creeley, *Contexts*, p. 21.

27. Ibid., p. 21.

28. Ibid., p. 5.

29. Robert Creeley, "The Art of Poetry," interview by Linda Wagner and Lewis MacAdams, Jr., *The Paris Review* 11, no. 44 (1968):172. When Olson went to Yucatán he wrote to Creeley almost daily. Creeley edited roughly one-fourth of these letters and published them in *Mayan Letters*.

30. Creeley, *Contexts*, p. 63.

31. Ibid., p. 11.

32. Creeley briefly outlines the history of Black Mountain College in an interview with Charles Tomlinson (*Contexts*, pp. 24–25).

33. Charles Olson, *Letters for Origin 1950–1956*, ed. Albert Glover (London: Cape Goliard Press, 1970), p. 87.

34. Ibid., p. 133. "The Black Mt. Quarterly" was subsequently called *Black Mountain Review* and became a biannual beginning with issue no. 5 in 1955. This publication should not be confused with *The Black Mountain Review* which began and ended with its first issue in June 1951.

35. Letter of 1 January 1956, at Yale University.

36. *Paris Review* interview, p. 170.

37. Creeley, *Contexts*, p. 69.

38. As cited by Novik, "Robert Creeley," p. 109.

39. Hugh Kenner, "More Than Pretty Music," *National Review*, 19 November 1960, p. 320.

40. Kenneth Rexroth, "Bearded Barbarians or Real Bards?," *The New York Times Book Review,* 12 February 1961, p. 44.

41. Richard Howard, *Alone with America* (New York: Atheneum Publishers, 1971), p. 66.

42. Robert Duncan, *"For Love,* by Robert Creeley," *New Mexico Quarterly* 32 (1962–63):219.

43. John William Corrington, "Creeley's *For Love:* Two Responses," *Northwest Review* 6 (1963):106.

44. As cited by Howard, *Alone With America,* p. 66.

45. Kenner, "More Than Pretty Music," p. 320.

46. Rexroth, "Bearded Barbarians or Real Bards?," p. 44.

47. As cited by Duncan, *"For Love,* by Robert Creeley," p. 219.

48. Ibid.

49. Ian Hamilton, *A Poetry Chronicle* (New York: Harper & Row Publishers, 1973), p. 163.

50. M. L. Rosenthal, "Problems of Robert Creeley," *Parnassus* (Fall/Winter 1973): 209–10.

51. Kenneth Cox. "Address and Posture in the Poetry of Robert Creeley," *Cambridge Quarterly* 4 (1969):243.

52. Louis Zukofsky, "What I Come to Do is Partial," *Poetry* 92 (1958):110.

53. Gilbert Sorrentino, "The Darkness Surrounds Us," *Poetry* 116 (1970):114.

54. Jerome Mazzaro, "Integrities," *Kenyon Review* 32 (1970):163.

55. Hamilton, *A Poetry Chronicle,* pp. 162, 163.

56. William Dickey, "On Robert Creeley," *Poetry* 101 (1963):422.

57. Creeley, *Contexts,* p. 184.

58. Ibid., p. 4.

59. As cited by Fielding Dawson, "On Creeley's Third Change," *Athanor* 4 (1973):58.

60. Albert Glover, "Letters for *Origin*" (Ph.D. diss., State University of New York at Buffalo, 1968), p. 76. The material cited does not appear in the published edition of this dissertation.

61. Charles Olson, *Human Universe and Other Essays,* ed. Donald Allen (New York: Grove Press, 1967), p. 4.

62. Paul Valéry, *Monsieur Teste,* trans. Jackson Mathews (Princeton: Princeton University Press, 1973). This summary of Teste's "system of self-awareness" is a compilation of his remarks which are scattered throughout the preface, ten chapters, and appendix of Valéry's novel.

63. Ibid., p. 77.

64. Creeley, *Contexts,* p. 198.

CHAPTER 1

1. Creeley, *Contexts,* p. 167.

2. Ibid.

3. In the summer of 1957, Migrant Books of Worcester, England, published Creeley's book of selected poems, *The Whip.* The poems had been selected by Creeley from his five earlier books of poetry: *Le Fou* (1952), *The Kind of Act of* (1953), *The Immoral Proposition* (1953), *A Snarling Garland* (1954), and *All That Is Lovely in Men* (1955). With the exception of "The Charm," all the poems in *The Whip* were reprinted in Part 1 of *For Love: Poems 1950–1960.* (New York: Charles Scribner's Sons, 1962).

4. Creeley, *Contexts,* p. 138.

5. Jean Hytier, *The Poetics of Paul Valéry*, trans. Richard Howard (New York: Doubleday & Co., Anchor Books, 1966), p. 284.

6. All citations in text in this chapter are to *For Love: Poems 1950–1960* (New York: Charles Scribner's Sons, 1962).

7. Creeley, *A Quick Graph*, pp. 75–87 and pp. 85–91, respectively.

8. Charles Olson, *Selected Writings of Charles Olson*, ed. Robert Creeley (New York: New Directions, 1966), p. 17.

9. Creeley, *Contexts*, p. 152. In an interview with Lewis MacAdams, Creeley recalled:

> . . . in these days, I remember, in the Cedars I had a big wooden handled clasp knife, that in moments of frustration and rage—I mean I never struck anybody with it, but it was, like I'd get that knife, you know, and I don't think I tried to scare people with it, but it was like, when all else failed, that knife was . . . not simply in the sense I was going to kill somebody, like a gun, but I loved that knife. You could carve things with it, make things and so on. And so, I'd apparently been flourishing it in the bar at some point, and I remember he took it away from me, John did, and he kept it and said, you know, like, "You're not going to have this knife for two weeks." And then he finally said, "Look, you can't come in here anymore." And I said, like, "What am I going to do? Where am I going to go?" So he would finally admit me if I drank ginger ale only. Because I used to stand out front and look in the window. And then he would let me come in and sit, as long as I was a good boy and drank only ginger ale. And finally he let me have the knife back, because that knife was very, very—I've still got one like it.

10. Ibid., p. 151.

11. Cid Corman's *Origin* 7 (1952) was in large part given over to translations of Benn's poems and to essays about them. This issue touched off a controversy over editorial policy with Corman on one side and Olson and Creeley on the other. Note Olson's letter to Corman dated 26 January 1953 (*Letters for Origin*, p. 116). When Creeley wrote "The Dishonest Mailmen" early in 1953, the Benn issue was very much in mind. Creeley's poem can be read as an extension of the argument that all but broke his faith in Corman.

12. "Talking on Your Notes."

13. *Monsieur Teste*, p. 25, 27.

14. Ibid., p. 103.

15. As cited in *The Poetics of Paul Valéry*, p. 44.

16. Ibid., p. 42.

17. Ibid., p. 47.

18. *"For Love*, by Robert Creeley," p. 222.

19. Marie Henri Beyle [Stendhal], *On Love*, trans. Philip Sidney Woolf (New York: Bretano's, n.d.), introduction, unnumbered.

20. Robert Duncan, *"For Love*, by Robert Creeley," p. 222. Duncan goes on to say that Robert Graves's *The White Goddess* plays its part here although Creeley, unlike Graves, does not "insist on a system" (p. 223). For Graves, the white goddess was the mother, the beloved *femme fatale*, and the old crone. Living on Mallorca, Creeley could not have failed to think about Graves's poetic theories. He used Graves for the prototype of the established poet in *The Island*.

21. In his Introduction to *Black Mountain Review* (p. vi), Creeley comments on his friendship with Rainer Gerhardt:

> One, *Fragmente*, edited and published in Freiberg, Germany by Rainer Gerhardt —whose acquaintance I was also to make through Pound's help—was an heroically ambitious attempt to bring back into the German literary canon all that writing which the years of the Third Reich had absented from it. Rainer and his wife, living in great poverty with two young sons, were nonetheless able to introduce to the German context an incredible range of work, including that of Olson, Williams,

Pound, Bunting, and myself . . . . Their conception of what such a magazine *might* accomplish was a deep lesson to me.

In 1950, Creeley became *Fragmente's* American editor, although the magazine folded before an American issue could be printed. See also "Rainer Gerhardt: A Note" (*A Quick Graph*, pp. 221–23). Note, too, Olson's "To Gerhardt, there among Europe's things of which he has written us in his 'Brief an Creeley und Olson' " and "The Death of Europe" (a funeral poem for Rainer M. Gerhardt). Olson's poems, like Creeley's "For Rainer Gerhardt," illustrate the tendency of the poets first associated with *Origin* and later with *Black Mountain Review* to refer to each other in their work. That Gerhardt was unknown to Creeley's readers does not overturn my comment that Creeley was able to deal with male friendship in straightforward terms from the start of his career.

22. John Constable, "The Poems of Robert Creeley," *Cambridge Review*, 15 October 1966, pp. 27, 28.

23. *"For Love*, by Robert Creeley," p. 221.

24. Warren Tallman, "Sunny Side Up: A Note on Robert Creeley," *Athanor* 4 (1973):64, 65.

25. Ibid.

26. "More than Pretty Music," p. 320. Kenner cites this poem and goes on to say that the volume *A Form of Women* is very likely one of the books for which everyone will be combing secondhand lists in ten years [1970]."

27. Jerome Mazzaro, "Robert Creeley, the Domestic Muse, and Post-Modernism," *Athanor* 4 (1973):28–29. Mazarro makes these comments about Creeley's mode of self-exploration in "The Hero" and "A Gift of Great Value."

28. Creeley, *A Quick Graph*, p. 112.

29. Corrington, "Creeley's *For Love:* Two Responses," pp. 109–10.

30. Duncan, "For Love," by Robert Creeley," p. 220.

31. Howard, *Alone with America*, p. 70.

32. Creeley, *Contexts*, p. 166.

33. Ibid., p. 167.

CHAPTER 2

1. *Words* (New York: Charles Scribner's Sons, 1967), p. 34. Other quotations from *Words* are cited by page in the text.

2. M. L. Rosenthal, *The Modern Poets* (New York: Oxford University Press, 1960), p. 268.

3. *Monsieur Teste*, p. 120.

4. Olson, *Selected Writings*, pp. 16–17.

5. Creeley, *Contexts*, p. 42.

6. Ibid.

7. Ibid., p. 41.

8. Ibid., p. 50.

9. Ibid., pp. 41–42.

10. Ibid., p. 50.

11. Ibid., p. 112.

12. *The Collected Books of Jack Spicer*, ed. Robin Blaser (Los Angeles: Black Sparrow Press, 1975), p. 132.

13. Walt Whitman, *Whitman Selected by Robert Creeley* (Baltimore: Penguin Books, Poet to Poet series, 1973), p. 12.

14. Ibid., p. 10.

15. Ibid., p. 13.

16. Ibid., p. 15.

CHAPTER 3

1. *Pieces* (New York: Charles Scribner's Sons, 1969), p. 58. All citations in the text of this chapter are to this volume.

2. Louis Zukofsky, *Ferdinand* (London: Grossman Publishers, 1968), p. 9.

3. Robert Creeley, "A Note on Louis Zukofsky," *A 1–12* (New York: Doubleday & Co., 1967), p. vii.

4. Creeley, *A Quick Graph*, p. 64.

5. Allen Ginsberg, *Allen Verbatim*, ed. Gordon Ball, (New York: McGraw-Hill, 1974), p. 25.

6. Creeley, *A Quick Graph*, p. 323.

7. Creeley refers to Duncan's poem "OFTEN I AM PERMITTED TO RETURN TO A MEADOW" where he finds described a distinct and definite place he also recognizes and values. Duncan's poem begins:

> OFTEN I AM PERMITTED TO
> RETURN TO A MEADOW
>
> as if it were a scene made-up by the mind,
> that is not mine, but is a made place,
>
> that is mine, it is so near to the heart,
> an eternal pasture folded in all thought
> so that there is a hall therein
>
> that is a made place, created by light
> wherefrom the shadows that are forms fall.

Creeley proposes in an interview that this commonly shared belief in an "obedience to a presence" accounted for the friendship among the "so-called Black Mountain writers" who as individual artists differed greatly: "I think it was simply the insistent feeling we were given something to write, that it was an obedience we were undertaking to an actual possibility of revelation" (*Contexts*, pp. 184–85).

8. Creeley, *Contexts*, p. 169.

9. Ibid., p. 202.

10. Martin Buber, *I and Thou* (New York: Charles Scribner's Sons, 1958).

CHAPTER 4

1. M. L. Rosenthal, "Problems of Robert Creeley," *Parnassus* 2 (1972–73):205.

2. Aram Saroyan, "An Extension of Content," *Poetry* 104 (1964):46.

3. Creeley, *A Quick Graph*, p. 124. Creeley is describing Louis Zukofsky's attitude with which he feels an affinity.

4. William Carlos Williams, *A Voyage to Pagany*, introduction by Harry Levin (New York: New Directions, 1970), p. xi.

5. *A Voyage to Pagany*, p. 15.

6. Citations in the text of this chapter are to Robert Creeley, *A Day Book* (New York: Scribners, 1972), unnumbered.

7. *A Voyage to Pagany*, pp. xvii, and xvi.

8. Ibid., p. xiv.

9. Creeley, *A Quick Graph*, p. 12.

10. Citations in this text of the 1967 preface are to Robert Creeley, *The Charm* (San Francisco: Four Seasons Foundation, 1969).

11. Creeley, *Contexts*, p. 42.

12. Ibid., p. 192.

13. Ibid., p. 42.

14. Ibid., 193.

15. Ibid., p. 192.

16. Denise Levertov. *The Poet in the World*, (New York: New Directions, 1973), pp. 239–40.

17. Charles Olson, *Selected Writings*, p. 16.

18. John Tytell, *Naked Angels: The Lives and Literature of the Beat Generation* (New York: McGraw Hill, 1976), p. 214.

19. As quoted by Tytell, *Naked Angels*, p. 199.

20. Ibid., p. 115. Burroughs learned the "cut-up" mosaic technique from Brion Gysin who tape recorded a message that became a touchstone for him:

> I come to free the words
> The words are free to come
> I come freely to the words
> The free come to the words

The similarity between the passage associated with Burroughs and the "small dreams" passage in "In London" seems too close to be unintentional.

21. Creeley, *Contexts*, p. 26.

22. Ibid., p. 21.

23. Robert Creeley, "From the Forest of Language: A Conversation with Robert Creeley," ed. Philip L. Gerber, *Athanor* 4 (1973):10. Gerber asked Creeley to describe "Creeley poetry." He answered:

> In my own rather semi-conscious understanding of what it's like, my poetry tends to be often in the emotional situation of being "uptight." It's nervous. In fact, at times, when I read, people assume that I'm in a highly nervous state, because the poetry sounds of this order. But when I was still quite young, just beginning thus to write, Charles Olson pointed out to me one of my dilemmas. In trying to achieve an effective line, I was extending it—the result of my interest in Wallace Stevens and respect for him—in ways that my own energy couldn't sustain. I tended to speak in a short, intensive manner. My thought, the line of my thought, Olson generously said, was rather long; but the statement of my thought was characteristically short and intensive. Olson had never met me at this time. He was getting this completely from the characteristic letters and writing I was sending him."

24. Creeley, *Contexts*, p. 193.

25. Gerber, "From the Forest of Language: A Conversation with Robert Creeley," p. 12.

26. Creeley, *Contexts*, p. 7. Creeley suggests his indebtedness to Jackson Pollock and John Cage.

27. Ibid., p. 193. Creeley is speaking here about the poems in *Pieces*. The same is true about the poems of "In London."

28. Charles Olson, *Letters for Origin: 1950–1956*, p. 87.

29. "People," first published in a single-poem volume titled *1.2.3.4.5.6.7.8.9.0* (Berkeley: Shambala; and San Francisco: Mundra, 1971), is dedicated to the artist Arthur Okamura. Okamura's eighteen delightful drawings of "little people" in the shapes of flowers, letters of the alphabet, and the like accompany the stanzas. Apart from being of interest in their own right, Okamura's designs remedy the misemphasis on the serious in "People" by illustrating the whimsical element inherent in the ideas the poem presents. "People," as it appears in "In London," suffers without them. Incidentally, it would seem that the name of this handsome ninety-page volume would refer more appropriately to "Numbers" (*Pieces*), a poem Creeley wrote at the suggestion of Robert Indiana (*Contexts*, p. 201) and dedicated to him.

30. Creeley also used the phrase "the stain of love" in one of his earliest poems inspired by his unhappy first marriage. In both "The Edge" (1971) and "Love" ('Not enough.') (1951), Creeley makes much of the phrase he borrowed from Williams's "Love Song." Whereas in Williams's poem, the deliciously sensuous "honey thick stain" suffuses "the colors/ of the whole world," bathing the world in love, in both of Creeley's poems "the stain of love" refers to sexuality as a blight, literally as "the stain."

31. As quoted by Jerome Mazzaro, "Robert Creeley, the Domestic Muse, and Post-Modernism," p. 23.

32. Gerber, "From the Forest of Language: A Conversation with Robert Creeley," p. 14.

33. Robert Creeley, "The Creative," *Sparrow* 6 (1973), unnumbered.

BIBLIOGRAPHY

MAJOR WORKS BY ROBERT CREELEY

The Gold Diggers and Other Stories. Mallorca: Divers Press, 1954; New York: Charles Scribner's Sons, 1965.

For Love: Poems 1950–1960. New York: Charles Scribner's Sons, 1962.

The Island. New York: Charles Scribner's Sons, 1963.

Words. New York: Charles Scribner's Sons, 1967.

The Charm: Early and Uncollected Poems. San Francisco: Four Seasons Foundation, 1969.

Pieces. New York: Charles Scribner's Sons, 1969.

A Quick Graph: Collected Notes & Essays. Edited by Donald Allen. San Francisco: Four Seasons Foundation, 1970.

A Day Book. New York: Charles Scribner's Sons, 1972.

Contexts of Poetry: Interviews 1961–1971. Edited by Donald Allen. Bolinas: Four Seasons Foundation, 1973.

Listen. Los Angeles: Black Sparrow Press, 1973.

WRITING WHOLLY OR PARTIALLY ABOUT ROBERT CREELEY

Altieri, Charles. "The Unsure Egoist: Robert Creeley and the Theme of Nothingness." *Contemporary Literature* 13 (1972):162–85.

Bly, Robert [Crunk]. "The Work of Robert Creeley." *The Fifties* 2 (1959):10–21.

Bromige, David. "Creeley's *For Love:* Two Responses." *Northwest Review* 6 (1963):110–122.

Cameron, Allen Barry. " 'Love Comes Quietly': The Poetry of Robert Creeley." *Chicago Review* 19 (1967):92–103.

Carroll, Paul. *The Poem in Its Skin.* Chicago: Follett Publishing Co., 1968.

Charters, Samuel. *Some Poems/Poets: Studies in American Underground Poetry Since 1945.* Berkeley: Oyez, 1971.

Chung, Ling. "Predicaments in Robert Creeley's *Words.*" *Concerning Poetry* 2 (1969): 32–35.

Constable, John. "The Poems of Robert Creeley." *Cambridge Review* 89 (1966):27–29.

Corrington, John. "Creeley's *For Love:* Two Responses." *Northwest Review* 6 (1963):106–10.

Cox, Kenneth. "Address and Posture in the Poetry of Robert Creeley." *Cambridge Quarterly* 4 (1969):237–43.

Dawson, Fielding. "On Creeley's Third Change." *Athanor* 4 (1973): 57–58.

Dickey, William. "Reticences of Pattern." *Poetry* 101 (1963):421–24.

Duncan, Robert. *"For Love* by Robert Creeley." *New Mexico Quarterly* 32 (1962–63):219–24.

Ellman, Richard, and O'Clair, Robert, editors. *The Norton Anthology of Modern Poetry.* New York: W. W. Norton & Co., 1973.

Hassan, Ihab. *Contemporary American Literature: 1945–1972.* New York: Frederick Ungar Publishing, 1973.

Hamilton, Ian Finley. *A Poetry Chronicle.* New York: Harper & Row Publishers, 1973.

Hoffman, Frederick J. *Patterns of Commitment in American Literature.* Edited by Marston La France. Toronto: University of Toronto Press, 1967.

181

Howard, Richard. *Alone With America.* New York: Atheneum Publishers, 1971.

Kenner, Hugh. "More Than Pretty Music." *National Review,* November 19, 1960, pp. 320–21.

Levertov, Denise. *The Poet in the World.* New York: New Directions, 1973.

Malkoff, Karl. *Crowell's Handbook of Contemporary American Poetry.* New York: Thomas Y. Crowell Co., 1973.

Mandel, Ann. *Measures: Robert Creeley's Poetry.* Toronto: Coach House Press, 1974.

Martz, Louis L. "Recent Poetry: The End of an Era." *Yale Review* 59 (1969):252–67.

Mazzaro, Jerome. "Integrities." *Kenyon Review* 32 (1970):163–68.

———. "Robert Creeley, the Domestic Muse, and Post-Modernism." *Athanor* 4 (1973):16–33.

Messing, Gordon M. "The Linguistic Analysis of Some Contemporary Nonformal Poetry." *Language and Style* 2 (1969):323–29.

Moon, Samuel. "Creeley as Narrator." *Poetry* 108 (1966):341–42.

McGann, Jerome. "Poetry and Truth." *Poetry* 117 (1970):195–203.

Novik, Mary. "A Creeley Chronology." *Athanor* 4 (1973):67–75.

———. *Robert Creeley: An Inventory, 1945–1970.* Kent, Ohio: Kent State University Press, 1973.

Olson, Charles. *Human Universe and Other Essays.* Edited by Donald Allen. New York: Grove Press, 1967.

Rexroth, Kenneth. "Bearded Barbarians or Real Bards?" *New York Times Book Review,* 12 February 1961, pp. 1, 44.

Rosenthal, M. L. "In Exquisite Chaos." *The Nation,* 1 November 1958, p. 327.

———. *The New Poets: American and British Poetry Since World War II.* New York: Oxford University Press, 1967.

———. "Problems of Robert Creeley." *Parnassus* 2 (1972):205–14.

Saroyan, Aram. "An Extension of Content." *Poetry* 104 (1964):45–47.

Sorrentino, Gilbert. "The Darkness Surrounds Us." *Poetry* 116 (1970):110–20.

Stepanchev, Stephen. *American Poetry Since 1945: A Critical Survey.* New York: Harper & Row Publishers, 1967.

Tallman, Warren. "Robert Creeley's Rimethought," *Tish,* no. 33, 4 January 1966, pp. 2–10. Reprinted in *A Nosegay in Black* 1, no. 1 (1966).

———. "Sunny Side Up: A Note on Robert Creeley." *Athanor* 4 (1973):64–66.

Wagner, Linda. "The Poet as Novelist: Creeley's Novel." *Critique* 7 (1964–65):119–22.

———. "The Latest Creeley." *American Poetry Review* 4 (1975):42–4.

Whittemore, Reed. "*Pieces* by Robert Creeley." *The New Republic,* 11 October 1969, p. 25.

Will, Frederick. "To Take Place and to 'Take Heart.' " *Poetry* 111 (1968):256–58.

Weatherhead, A. Kingsley. *The Edge of the Image.* Seattle and London: University of Washington Press, 1967.

Zukofsky, Louis. "What I Come To Do is Partial." *Poetry* 92 (1958):110–12.

SELECTED MISCELLANEOUS WRITINGS

Allen, Donald M., and Creeley, Robert, eds., *New American Story.* New York: Grove Press, 1965.

Buber, Martin. *I and Thou.* New York: Charles Scribner's Sons, 1958.

Beyle, Marie Henri [Stendhal]. *On Love.* Translated by Philip Sidney Woolf. New York: Brentano's, n.d.

Cage, John. *Silence: Lectures and Writings by John Cage.* Middletown, Connecticut: Wesleyan University Press, 1973.

Cook, Bruce. *The Beat Generation.* New York: Charles Scribner's Sons, 1971.

Crane, Hart. *The Complete Poems and Selected Letters and Prose of Hart Crane.* Edited by Brom Weber. New York: Doubleday & Co., Anchor Books, 1966.

————. *The Letters of Hart Crane: 1916–1932*. Edited by Brom Weber. New York: Heritage Press, 1952.

Creeley, Robert. "The Art of Poetry," interview conducted by Linda Wagner and Lewis MacAdams, Jr. *Paris Review* 11 (1968):155–87.

————. "At Placitas." Interview with author. May 1975.

————. *The Creative*. Los Angeles: Black Sparrow Press, 1973.

————. "From the Forest of Language: A Conversation with Robert Creeley." Interview conducted by Philip Gerber with Jerome Mazzaro. *Athanor* 4 (1973):9–15.

————. "Introduction." *Black Mountain Review*, reprint edition. New York: A.M.S. Reprint, 1969, pp. iii–xiii.

————. "Introduction." *New Writing in the U.S.A.* Edited by Robert Creeley and Donald M. Allen. Harmondsworth, England: Penguin Books, 1967.

————. "Introduction." *Whitman Selected by Robert Creeley*. Harmondsworth, England: Penguin Books, 1973.

————. Letter to Vincent Ferrini, 29 March 1950. *Athanor* 4 (1973):59–60.

————. Letter to William Carlos Williams, 1 January 1957, at Yale University.

————. "Talking on Your Notes." Tape prepared for author. August, 1975.

Davie, Donald. *Articulate Energy*. New York: Harcourt, Brace and Co., 1955.

Dawson, Fielding. *The Black Mountain Book*. New York: Croton Press, 1970.

Dembo, L. S. *Conceptions of Reality in Modern American Poetry*. Berkeley and Los Angeles: University of California Press, 1966.

Duberman, Martin. *Black Mountain College: An Exploration in Community*. New York: E. P. Dutton & Co., 1972.

Fenollosa, Ernest. *The Chinese Written Character as a Medium for Poetry*. Edited by Ezra Pound. San Francisco: City Lights Books, 1964.

Frye, Northrop. *Anatomy of Criticism: Four Essays*. Princeton: Princeton University Press, 1957.

Ginsberg, Allen. *Allen Verbatim*. Edited by Gordon Ball. New York: McGraw-Hill, 1974.

Glover, Albert. "Charles Olson: Letters for *Origin*." Ph.D. Dissertation, State University of New York at Buffalo, 1968.

Hall, Donald, ed. *Contemporary American Poetry*. Baltimore: Penguin Books, 1962.

Hytier, Jean. *The Poetics of Paul Valéry*. Translated by Richard Howard. New York: Doubleday & Co., 1966.

Ince, W. N. *The Poetic Theory of Paul Valéry: Inspiration and Technique*. Paris: Leicester University Press, 1961.

Kenner, Hugh. *The Pound Era*. Berkeley and Los Angeles: University of California Press, 1971.

————. *A Homemade World: The American Modernist Writers*. New York: William Morrow and Co., 1975.

Ker, W. P. *Epic and Romance: Essays on Medieval Literature*. London: Macmillan and Co., 1908.

Kerouac, Jack. "Essentials of Spontaneous Prose." *Black Mountain Review* 7 (1957):226–28.

Miller, J. Hillis., ed. *William Carlos Williams: A Collection of Critical Essays*. Englewood Cliffs, New Jersey: Prentice-Hall, 1966.

Olson, Charles. *Archaeologist of Morning*. New York: Cape Golliard/Grossman, 1971.

————. *The Distances*. New York: Grove Press, 1960.

————. *Letters for Origin: 1950–1956*. Edited by Albert Glover. New York: Cape Golliard/Grossman, 1970.

————. *Mayan Letters*. Edited by Robert Creeley. Mallorca: Divers Press, 1953; London: Jonathan Cape, 1968.

————. *The Maximus Poems*. New York: Jargon/Corinth, 1960.

————. *Maximus Poems IV, V, VI*. New York: Grossman Publishers, 1968.

————. *Pleistocene Man: A Curriculum For The Study Of The Soul.* New York: Institute of Further Studies, 1968.

————. *Selected Writings of Charles Olson.* Edited by Robert Creeley. New York: New Directions, 1966.

Ossman, David, ed. *The Sullen Art.* New York: Corinth, 1963.

Pound, Ezra. *ABC of Reading.* New York: New Directions, 1960.

————. *The Cantos of Ezra Pound.* New York: New Directions, 1970.

————. *A Guide to Kulchur.* New York: New Directions, 1938.

————. *Literary Essays of Ezra Pound.* Edited by T. S. Eliot. New York: New Directions, 1968.

Reck, Michael. *Ezra Pound: A Close-Up.* New York: McGraw-Hill, 1967.

Reed, Edward Bliss. *English Lyrical Poetry: From Its Origins To the Present Time.* New York: Haskell House, 1967.

Rexroth, Kenneth. *American Poetry in the Twentieth Century.* New York: Seabury Press, 1973.

Sartre, Jean-Paul. *The Psychology of Imagination.* New Jersey: Citadel Press, 1972.

————. *What Is Literature?* Translated by Bernard Frechtman. New York: Harper & Row Publishers, 1965.

————. *The Words.* Translated by Bernard Frechtman. New York: George Braziller, 1964.

Sewell, Elizabeth. *Paul Valéry: The Mind In The Mirror.* New Haven: Yale University Press, 1952.

Spicer, Jack. *The Collected Books of Jack Spicer.* Edited by Robin Blaser. Los Angeles: Black Sparrow Press, 1975.

Stevens, Wallace. *The Collected Poems.* New York: Alfred A. Knopf, 1954.

Suckling, Norman. *Paul Valéry and The Civilized Mind.* London: Oxford University Press, 1954.

Trilling, Lionel. *Mind in the Modern World.* New York: Viking Press, 1972.

Tytell, John. *Naked Angels: The Lives and Literature of the Beat Generation.* New York: McGraw-Hill, 1976.

Valéry, Paul. *Monsieur Teste.* Translated by Jackson Mathews. Princeton: Princeton University Press, 1973.

Waggoner, Hyatt H. *American Poets: From the Puritans to the Present.* Boston: Houghton Mifflin Co., 1968.

Waite, Arthur. *A Pictorial Guide to the Tarot.* New York: University Books, 1959.

Walsh, Chad. *Today's Poets: American and British Poetry Since the 1930's.* New York: Charles Scribner's Sons, 1964.

Williams, William Carlos. *The Collected Earlier Poems of William Carlos Williams.* New York: New Directions, 1951.

————. *The Collected Later Poems of William Carlos Williams.* New York: New Directions, 1963.

————. *In The American Grain.* Connecticut: New Directions, 1925.

————. *Paterson.* New York: New Directions, 1963.

————. *Selected Essays of William Carlos Williams.* New York: Random House, 1954.

————. *Spring and All.* San Francisco: Frontier Press, 1970.

————. *A Voyage to Pagany.* New York: New Directions, 1970.

Zukofsky, Louis. *A.* 2 vols. New York: Doubleday & Co., 1967.

————. *All: The Collected Short Poems 1923–1958.* New York: W. W. Norton and Co., 1965.

————. *Bottom: On Shakespeare.* 2 vols. Austin: Ark Press for University of Texas Press, 1963.

————. *Ferdinand.* London: Grossman Publishers, 1968.

————. *Prepositions: The Collected Critical Essays of Louis Zukofsky.* New York: Horizon Press, 1968.

INDEX OF TITLES

185